TWAYNE'S WORLD AUTHORS SERIES
A Survey of the World's Literature

FRANCE

Maxwell A. Smith, Guerry Professor of French, Emeritus
The University of Chattanooga
Former Visiting Professor in Modern Languages
The Florida State University
EDITOR

Pierre Reverdy

TWAS 567

Pierre Reverdy

PIERRE REVERDY

By JEAN SCHROEDER

TWAYNE PUBLISHERS
A DIVISION OF G. K. HALL & CO., BOSTON

Copyright © 1981 by G. K. Hall & Co.

Published in 1981 by Twayne Publishers,
A Division of G. K. Hall & Co.
All Rights Reserved

Printed on permanent/durable acid-free paper and bound
in the United States of America

First Printing

Library of Congress Cataloging in Publication Data
Schroeder, Jean.
Pierre Reverdy.
(Twayne's world authors series ; TWAS 567 : France)
Bibliography: p. 168–73
Includes index.
1.   Reverdy, Pierre, 1889-1960—Criticism and interpretation.
PQ2635.E85Z87   841'.912   80-19301
ISBN 0-8057-6409-7

To Robert and Eric

Contents

About the Author

Jean Schroeder holds the B.A. degree from Elmira College, the M.S. degree from Georgetown University, and the M.A. and Ph.D. degrees from the Graduate Center of the City University of New York. She was elected to Phi Beta Kappa as an undergraduate and spent a year studying at the Sorbonne. She has been a lecturer in French at Queens College in New York where she taught undergraduate courses in French grammar and literature.

Besides French literature, she has also taught English grammar and American culture, and has recently published an English grammar text.

Preface

Reverdy speculated that the writer, at the moment of composition, had no clear idea of his intent or meaning, but instead gave way to an image or poetic figure which his mind, upon reflection, had helped to shape and fashion.[1] The significance of ideas and, moreover, of events and circumstances, could escape the creator, for whom they had no tangible reality until some indefinite time in the future. This book, then, does not seek to analyze definitively Reverdy's work, but instead offers possible explanations of imagery, theme, and artistic motivation. Discussion of Reverdy's work is, for the most part, centered upon his preferred leitmotiv, the wanderings of an anonymous traveler whose objective and destination are never clearly defined. Wayfaring would seem to offer the traveler unlimited freedom; however, as Reverdy himself points out, images of restriction permanently block some paths, while others paradoxically open into settings of disorienting void.

The theme of the voyage, for Reverdy and several other French poets, is usually associated with the cycle of descent/ascent. Descriptions during the journeys of Reverdy's voyager frequently bring to mind the work of three poets of the nineteenth century, Baudelaire, Mallarmé, and Rimbaud. Baudelaire, indifferent as to whether the voyage is upward or downward, seeks only *le nouveau* ("the new"), in the hope of renewing his poetic inspiration: "Plonger au fond du gouffre, Enfer ou Ciel, qu'importe?/Au fond de l'Inconnu pour trouver du *nouveau!*" ("To dive to the bottom of the abyss, hell or heaven, of what importance?/To the depths of the unknown to find the *new!*").[2] For Mallarmé, the theme of the fall represents loss of self, i.e., the poet as an individual is destroyed, yet he achieves rebirth as the essence of poetry itself. Mallarmé's Igitur in the work of that name descends into the tomb, nullifying his entire existence but at the same time recreating himself as part of the realization of *the Infinite, the Absolute,* "le château de la pureté" ("the château of purity").[3] The journey upward, referred to in other poems such as "Les Fenêtres"

("The Windows"),[4] symbolizes the entrance into the azure, the realm of absolute artistic expression.

Rimbaud, unlike Baudelaire and Mallarmé, is preoccupied with the aspect of descent. Far from Mallarmé's realm of ideality, Rimbaud's destination is hell where the soul will undergo an exploration of the depths of its subconscious. Rimbaud's intent is to forcefully strip the self of its acquired social facades and to reveal its primitive nudity. Divested of earthly limitations, all forms of emotions are permitted, through disorder and immoderation, to reach their ultimate point. Through this long experience which Rimbaud calls "un long, immense et raisonné *dérèglement* de *tous les sens*" ("a long, boundless, and reasoned *disorder* of *all the senses*"), the objective, "l'*inconnu*" ("the *unknown*"), would be attained and the creative soul would come to know itself.[5] Reverdy, who frequently alludes to both descent and ascent in his poetry, recognizes the legacy of both Mallarmé and Rimbaud:

Du reste, il y a toujours eu, dans tous les arts, une double tentation à la bifurcation des pentes: la pente à gravir vers la hauteur sans air, l'esprit et la lumière (type Mallarmé) et la pente à descendre dans le gouffre obscur du sang, des sensations et de la chair (type Rimbaud).[6]

Moreover, there has always been, in all arts, a double temptation toward a branching of slopes: the slope to climb toward the height without air, the mind and light (Mallarmé's type) and the slope to descend into the dark abyss of blood, of sensations and of flesh (Rimbaud's type).

The analysis of the Reverdian voyage begins after a brief discussion of Reverdy's position with regard to the literary and art movements influencing his work as well as some relevant biographical details about his years in Paris and Solesmes. Following this introduction, the order of the chapters is chronological, each section first summarizing the basic characteristics of theme and style to be analyzed in the pages ahead. The fundamental themes and poetic figures recur from text to text, and I have tried to indicate variation and development by comparison and contrast. Owing to limitations of time and space, discussion must be restricted to the most important poems of each collection, the most essential passages of the prose works. As the reader will see, Reverdy was a prolific writer, leaving behind, in addition to a wealth of more known works, an abundance of articles relating mostly to aesthetics. I regret that a more detailed treatment of these was not possible; had more space been available, I would have preferred to give further attention to stylistic comments in the tradition of the *explication de texte*. Such undertakings will, no doubt, be carried out as the interest in Reverdy grows, especially in light of the republications of much of his work done by Flammarion, Gallimard, and Mercure de France.

Grateful thanks are to be offered to Professors Henri Peyre and Mary Ann Caws for their generous support and guidance. I am also indebted to the New York Public Library for its cooperation and assistance in the use of the Spencer and Arents Collections. Unless otherwise indicated, all translations are my own.

JEAN SCHROEDER

Los Angeles, California

Chronology

1889   September 13, Pierre Reverdy born in Narbonne.

1910   October 3, arrives in Paris.

1911   Becomes friendly with Georges Braque, Pablo Picasso, Juan Gris, and Henri Laurens.

1912   Employed by a newspaper as proofreader and typesetter. Becomes secretary to Adolphe Brisson. Friendship with Guillaume Apollinaire. Moves to Place Ravignan across from the Bateau-Lavoir.

1913   Begins *Cale sèche*.

1914   Enlists in auxiliary unit of the army although officially exempt from service.

1915   Completes *Cale sèche* which appears in *Main-d'oeuvre* in 1949. Publishes *Poèmes en prose* with illustrations by Juan Gris and Henri Laurens.

1916   Discharged from military service. *Quelques poèmes* and *La Lucarne ovale*.

1917   March 15, first issue of *Nord-Sud*, founded and directed by Reverdy. *Le Voleur de Talan*.

1918   *Les Ardoises du toit* and *Les Jockeys camouflés* appear, the latter illustrated by Henri Matisse. Last issue of *Nord-Sud* in October.

1919   Publishes *La Guitare endormie* with art work by Juan Gris and *Self defence*, dedicated to Gris.

1921   May 2, conversion to Catholicism. *Coeur de chêne* and *Etoiles peintes*.

1922   *Cravates de chanvre*.

1924   *Epaves du ciel*, an anthology composed of nine volumes of poetry. *Pablo Picasso et son oeuvre*.

1925   *Ecumes de la mer* (poems from *La Lucarne ovale*, *Les Ardoises du toit*, and *La Guitare endormie*) and *Grande nature*.

1926   May 30, retires to Solesmes. *La Peau de l'homme*.

1927   *Le Gant de crin*.

1928   *La Balle au bond*. Loss of religious faith.

1929   *Flaques de verre* and *Sources du vent*.
1930   *Pierres blanches* and *Risques et périls*, written between 1915 and 1928. Begins *Le Livre de mon bord*.
1936   Finishes *Le Livre de mon bord*.
1937   *Ferraille*.
1940   *Plein verre*.
1944   Begins to write *Le Chant des morts*.
1945   *Plupart du temps 1915–1922*, volumes 1–2.
1946   *Visages*, anthology of poems from *Sources du vent* and *Plein verre* with lithographs by Matisse. Begins *Bois vert*.
1948   *Le Livre de mon bord* and *Le Chant des morts*.
1949   *Bois vert* finished. *Main-d'oeuvre 1913–1949*.
1955   Publishes *Les Papiers collés de Laurens* and *Au soleil du plafond* with lithographs by Henri Laurens and Juan Gris respectively. Text of latter work probably composed by 1917.
1956   *En vrac*.
1960   Publishes *La Liberté des mers*, much of which was written during 1915–1916. June 17, Reverdy dies at Solesmes.

CHAPTER 1

The Artist and His Milieu

ALTHOUGH Pierre Reverdy's writing is not largely autobiographical, the reader may find a brief description of his epoch and milieu helpful in the appreciation of his work. Paris especially, together with the influence of the avant-garde art movements Reverdy encountered there, constitutes a pervasive presence throughout the earlier texts. Later, Solesmes' years of religious crisis contribute significantly to the themes of turmoil and holocaust prevalent in both prose and poetry. A complete biography is, however, impossible owing to the unavailability of material. The dearth of biographical information is perhaps attributable to the poet himself, who placed great value upon his personal privacy, indeed, spending much of his life as a recluse. Yet, although as a person Reverdy may have been aloof, he is quite accessible through his writing, particularly his poetry, in which he bares the agony and fragmentation of his spirit.

I Paris: Literary Apprenticeship and Direction

Reverdy's literary career began in Paris where he arrived on October 3, 1910. He was unaccustomed to the excitement and pace of city life, having been born in the small, provincial town of Narbonne on September 13, 1889. All that is known of his childhood is that he was raised in an anticlerical family of no chosen religious denomination. His father was a vine grower and vintner, his grandfather a sculptor.[1]

Upon arriving in Paris, Reverdy—with an affinity for art nourished perhaps by his grandfather's craft—chose to live among the leaders of what were to become several avant-garde movements. During the first two years he became friendly with the painters Georges Braque, Pablo Picasso, Juan Gris, the sculptor Henri Laurens, and the poets Guillaume Apollinaire, Max Jacob, Blaise Cendrars, and André Salmon. Reverdy lived on the Place Ravignan and frequented the Bateau-

Lavoir, a focal point where multitudes of artists converged to debate their respective causes célèbres. However, the early years in Paris were not entirely dedicated to literary debate and discussions. Some attention had to be given to the dreary but persistent problem of making a living. Reverdy was first employed as a proofreader and typesetter for a newspaper, later as a secretary.[2] Few indeed were the precious hours which he could devote to writing. Yet, perhaps the involuntary delay in composition was fortuitous, for by 1913, when he had already begun to write his first volume of poetry, *Cale sèche (Dry Dock)*, he had been exposed to the then dominant aesthetic currents, assimilating and further refining some, resolutely discarding others.

One of the strongest influences throughout Reverdy's early poetry was provided by the art movement known as cubism. The new generation of poets with which Reverdy allied himself viewed the declining symbolist movement with great disenchantment. Instead of the symbol and its implied withdrawal from reality, they chose the most quotidian objects in order to effect a return to the physical world.[3] The commonplace objects seen in cubist still lifes were drawn not for the purpose of imitation or objective representation, but rather as an illustration of the artist's conception of what newspapers, tables, guitars, etc. really looked like, when isolated from the dictates of society. Apollinaire, acting as spokesman for the cubist painters and poets in his *Chroniques d'art*, viewed cubist art as one based upon an interior, intellectual reality, as opposed to more traditional art, founded upon objective reality and perspective.[4]

Inspired by cubist doctrine and especially by his mentor Apollinaire,[5] Reverdy in *Cale sèche*, written during 1913–1915, echoed the prevailing disenchantment with the idealism of the symbolist school as well as with the emphasis upon objective representation advocated by traditional art. Moreover, the objects depicted in the cubist tableaux of Picasso, Braque, and Gris found their counterparts throughout Reverdy's early poetry, from the *Poèmes en prose (Prose Poems*, 1915) to *La Guitare endormie (The Guitar Asleep*, 1919). Many were the poems which described rooms and views from windows where the most modest, commonplace objects predominated—lamps, pipes, stairways, streets, mirrors. Reflecting the cubist objective to seek the independence of the object from fixed notions of physical reality, Reverdy undertook to separate the authentic, pure, semantic properties of words from arbitrary conventions. In this regard, he not only revealed the strong influence of cubism but also the rich heritage of Mallarmé.

Related to Reverdy's desire to realize the essence of words within a poem was his belief that the literary work created would become a new and independent object, a concrete reflection of an ideal.

It was again with the encouragement of Apollinaire and the cubist poet Max Jacob that Reverdy associated himself with two other avant-garde movements which also arose as reactions to symbolism: simultanism and futurism. Simultanism[6] was "the process of presenting without any transition events taking place at the same time but in different places."[7] The attempt "to render artistically the simultaneity and multiplicity of perceptual experience"[8] was supported first by the cinema, where varied elements of time and space were synthesized, and then, by the writing of Henri Bergson in which the phenomenon of memory operated outside of the realm of chronology.[9] Moreover, Braque and Picasso painted objects grouped in space which were not contingent upon temporality.[10] The poetry produced as a result of exposure to simultanism depicted successive views of a particular object and sought to capitalize upon the disorder of the interrupted perceptions.[11]

The futurist movement was introduced to France in a manifesto written by F. T. Marinetti and printed in *Le Figaro* in 1909. Less popular in France than in Italy where it had originated, it used the simultanist technique of rupture and multiple views to advocate new values—danger, conquest, speed, courage, war.[12] Reverdy never officially joined futurism nor, for that matter, cubism, and indeed, he persistently denied that his work was either futurist or cubist in nature. However, traces of futurist influence are evident in several of the *Poèmes en prose*, reappearing later in *Les Jockeys camouflés* (*Disguised Jockeys*, 1918), in which various stages of movement were synthesized.

The Paris which had brought Reverdy into the mainstream of the avant-garde lay almost barren by 1916; the dedicated artists and their controversial expositions had been swept into the turmoil of World War I. Reverdy had already declared himself an antimilitarist and had been exempted earlier from military service. Yet, he too voluntarily enlisted in an auxiliary unit, only to be discharged in 1916.[13] By the end of that year, Apollinaire, severely wounded and also released, had come back to Paris. With his return Reverdy was to embark upon an experiment which further renewed his literary creativity.

The deepening friendship between the two poets instilled Reverdy with a sense of confidence in his craft, encouraging him in the spring of 1917 to found the literary review *Nord-Sud* (*North-South*). Its title was inspired by the subway line which connected the two major artistic communities, Montmartre and Montparnasse.[14] As editor in chief, Reverdy looked upon the review as an opportunity to unite two directions in poetry, the generation of 1914 and that of the post–World War I avant-garde. The former artistic group led by Apollinaire and supported by the cubists contributed their faith in the progress of the new century, while at the same time recognizing their presymbolist heritage, the thematic traditions of Baudelaire, Mallarmé, and Rimbaud, all of whom were to ultimately influence Reverdy. The latter poetic generation sought by their collaboration to announce new trends in poetry, first dada, founded by Tristan Tzara, and then surrealism, at that time a movement in embryonic form under the aegis of André Breton.[15] Yet, *Nord-Sud* was more than just an introduction to new directions in poetry; it provided Reverdy with a means of expression for many of his first aesthetic theories, most of which had been formed during his early years in Paris. In addition to his work on this review, Reverdy during the same year published his first novel, written in free verse, *Le Voleur de Talan* (*The Thief of Talan*).

As a literary experiment, *Nord-Sud* provided one of the richest periods in Reverdy's life. Its existence was, however, ephemeral, the last issue appearing in October, 1918.[16] It was during this same year that Reverdy published one of his more well-known collections of poetry, *Les Ardoises du toit* (*Slates of the Roof*). In the following year, there appeared another collection on aesthetics, *Self defence*, which included several expanded portions of essays from *Nord-Sud*, together with some new pieces. This collection was soon followed by another group of poems, *La Guitare endormie*, the last principal work inspired from the *Nord-Sud* era. Hereafter, the majority of Reverdy's work reflected a new type of atmosphere, one of deep psychological and religious crisis.

As the *Nord-Sud* epoch closed, Max Jacob, who had helped to acquaint Reverdy with the literary forces of the period, now turned his attention to matters of religion. It was Jacob, himself a recent convert to Catholicism, who retired to the Benedictine abbey at Saint-Benoît-sur-Loire, and who sought, through his own religious experience, to urge Reverdy and his wife to join him. Although Reverdy and Jacob had often quarreled, Reverdy was impressed by Jacob's religious fervor and evangelism, and as a result, he and his wife converted to Catholicism in 1921. Five years later, Reverdy, like Jacob, decided to pursue a life more oriented toward God as well as poetry; he and his wife retired to the monastery of Solesmes. During the years just prior to Reverdy's seclusion, he published the collections *Coeur de chêne* (*Heart of Oak*), *Etoiles peintes* (*Painted Stars*, 1921), *Cravates de chanvre* (*Ties of Hemp*, 1922), *Grande nature* (*Sovereign Nature*, 1925), and two anthologies, *Epaves du ciel* (*Derelicts of Heaven*, 1924) and *Ecumes de la mer* (*Foam of the Sea*, 1925). The poetry of this particular period began to reflect the psychological uncertainty and turmoil that permeated his later work; only infrequent traces of cubism and futurism now remained.

II   *Solesmes: Seclusion and Disorientation*

It was on May 30, 1926, that Reverdy and his wife moved to Solesmes. Although he himself had completely lost his faith by the end of his second year there, he lived in seclusion at Solesmes for the remainder of his life. Reverdy's publications during the first years there traced the abruptness and contradiction within himself. *La Peau de l'homme* (*Man's Skin*), a novel and short stories, while published in 1926, was actually written during 1917–1922. It consequently showed little evidence of Reverdy's religious fervor and subsequent disillusionment. In contrast, however, was the atmosphere of religious enthusiasm and devotion found in *Le Gant de crin* (*Glove of Horsehair*), a work of 1927 which presented the poet's views on aesthetics as well as personal notes. His tone again abruptly changed in the last volume of poetry from this period, *La Balle au bond* (*Ball on the Bounce*), a work in which his ensuing skepticism, guilt, and despair were pervasive. After the year 1928, his poetry became more and more lugubrious, as if he wrote principally to purge himself of his metaphysical anxieties.

The peaceful solitude of Solesmes, unfortunately, did not provide Reverdy with the inner strength and motivation necessary to pursue a life of asceticism and piety. His religious ardor progressively subsided and eventually disappeared. Instead of a higher spiritual state, Reverdy experienced bitter resentment toward the church; religion as an institution was irreversibly tainted by human interpretation: "Man's great anxiety does not derive from death. Religions have greatly contributed in creating and aggravating it, religions with their sinister promises of good and evil, in any case, an eternal life in fire or honey."[17] His failure to find a spiritual ideal nurtured a vein of acrid pessimism that manifested itself in the poet's reaction to future involvement with the sec-

ular world: Reverdy envisioned himself a derelict cast out from the
fold, a victim of religious ambiguity condemned eternally to "this
uncertain and precarious journey upon the void."[18] Written in 1928
during the poet's acute disillusionment and included in the collection
Risques et périls (*Risks and Dangers*, 1930), the short story "Maison
hantée" ("Haunted House") re-created his fear of isolation and his
preoccupation with death and decomposition.

Reverdy's depression did not abate but instead deepened into feelings of intense persecution and deprivation. As might be expected,
when the poet's spiritual fervor had been consumed, his friendship
with Max Jacob badly deteriorated. It was at the same time that he
ceased to see another friend, Jean Cocteau. Although bitterly disillu-
sioned, Reverdy continued his self-appointed exile. Withdrawn from
the mainstream of avant-garde Paris, his work received decreasing
notice, a situation which further aggravated his depression. Meaningful
relationships with his fellowmen were impossible, he believed; even the
world of nature had turned against him: "Nature has appeared to me
as something hostile, inhuman, which opposes itself to man, causing
him terrible anguish; man is at grips with his environment."[19]

However, for Reverdy, even at his most lugubrious moments, there
was a modicum of hope which he never relinquished. Art represented
the means by which man might protest the alienation and absurdity of
his life; art was to be his only dignity, his only sustenance.[20] Assuming
the role of seer, the artist imagined existence as reduced to a void
inhabited by a solitary figure who vainly waited for orientation; art,
however, could make the wait seem shorter and more palatable: " . . .
that man is literally bored to death on earth and that he would certainly have died a long time ago, without a trace, if art had not come
to distract him."[21]

The poetry born of the poet's metaphysical torment and ensuing
pessimism constituted an appeal against the injustice of human alienation. Gone was the worship of equilibrium and stability encountered
earlier in *Le Gant de crin*, and in its place an emphasis upon change
was introduced. Published subsequent to the poet's metaphysical crisis,
Le Livre de mon bord (*My Journal*), a collection of meditations, bore
witness to his obsession with transformation: hereafter reality became
constant change, movement forever continuing.[22] Diffused throughout
the poetry of *Flaques de verre* (*Pools of Glass*), *Sources du vent*
(*Sources of the Wind*), both of 1929, and a collection published in
1930, *Pierres blanches* (*White Stones*), themes of motion were

expressed in images of physical fragmentation and inundation, in addition to intense psychological contradiction. Later on, with the publication of *Ferraille* (*Scrap Iron*, 1937), the most violent movement replaced simple transformation. Chaotic scenes of world holocaust and the disintegration of the poet's own psyche abounded. The themes of violence subsided somewhat with one of his last great volumes of poetry, *Le Chant des morts* (*Song of the Dead*), composed during the years 1944–1948. Resigned to the instability of human existence, the poet, in anticipation, depicted his own personal descent into the abyss from which there was to be no return. In many of the poems of *Plein verre* (*Full Glass*), published in 1940, and then in those of his last volume, *Bois vert* (*Green Wood*), finished in 1949, the profile of death was drawn in a total absence of motion, in a pure state of stagnation.

Yet, although constantly haunted by death, Reverdy, in one of his last works, *En vrac* (*In Bulk*, 1956), a collection of diverse aphorisms, continued to affirm his faith in art which had restored his life with a sense of identity and psychological stability. Poetry still represented a mitigating force against human finitude—"A hyphen in the finite which constantly ruptures (life is a continuous disintegration of matter and even of the finite spirit which are transformed) with the infinite, without deterioration."[23] Art ensured the poet a smooth transition from rupture in the sphere of the finite to continuity in the sphere of the infinite. Pierre Reverdy died at Solesmes on June 17, 1960.

CHAPTER 2

The Formative Years, 1913–1916

MUCH of Pierre Reverdy's early poetry attempts to reconcile the vestiges of romanticism and symbolism with the fundamental tenets of the then contemporary art movements of futurism, simultanism, and cubism. However, his first poetry must not be construed as merely a struggle between the forces of his literary heritage and those of avant-garde Paris in the years just prior to World War I. Underlying his efforts to reconcile and assimilate a motley collection of influences is a desire to forge for himself a new direction in poetry, even though this yearning is frequently riddled with self-doubt. Reverdy's first volume of poetry, *Cale sèche*, written during 1913–1915 but, curiously enough, not published until 1949, reveals his apprenticeship to the avant-garde and questions the wisdom of alignment with the past. The next two collections of poetry, *Poèmes en prose* and *Quelques poèmes* (*Several Poems*), written in 1915 and 1916 respectively, continue to reflect Reverdy's attempts to assimilate the tendencies of the avant-garde. At the end of the formative period, with the works *La Lucarne ovale* (*The Oval Garret Window*) and *La Liberté des mers* (*Freedom of the Seas*) Reverdy achieves much more individuality of theme and style, realizing aspects of his art that had appeared in only embryonic form in *Cale sèche*.

I   Cale sèche

The poet of *Cale sèche* (*Dry Dock*)[1] is hesitant and uncertain, caught between the onslaught of the past and the lure of the future. Aside from self-doubt and skepticism concerning the renewal of his poetic inspiration, he is preoccupied with the figure of line linked to the theme of voyage. Reverdy's voyagers throughout his poetry are all solitary, isolated figures, similarly indistinguishable. The temporal aspect of the voyage is treated in either evocations of death conceived in a vein of morose humor, in effect, a Baudelairian, spectral badinage, or in terms of accumulated past memories, most of which confuse the poet, compelling him to search deep within himself in order to decide what is to be discarded or retained. Directly associated with the idea of examination and purgation is the title of the collection, *Cale sèche*. The inner voyage or descent occurs below the level of one's consciousness, and is frequently presented in Reverdy's poetry by the image of the ship. The title *Dry Dock* would seem to suggest, then, that the ship has been laid up for repairs, so that when next put to sea, there will remain in the foam of its wake rich thematic material, the fruit of creative transformation.

A.   *Toward Creativity: A Trilogy*

Of the twenty-nine poems comprising *Cale sèche*, there are three long pieces which depict, in particular, the apprenticeship of the poet: the literary climate of Paris, Reverdy's preoccupation with the renewal of his poetic inspiration, and his concern with the specific direction his poetry should take. Characteristic of the entire volume, the three poems "Tentative," "Sujets," and "Bande de souvenirs" are punctuated only by interior rhythm and pauses in thought, containing very informal, if not frequently irregular rhyme schemes. The absence of formal punctuation, while perhaps not a direct influence of Apollinaire's revolutionary unpunctuated *Alcools* of 1913, is surely a product of the pre–World War I Parisian literary climate where, especially in poetry and art, established conventions were being challenged by new values and directions.

Reverdy's struggle to begin writing is presented in the poem "Tentative" ("Attempt") as a confrontation in the present between the past and the future. The fundamental metaphor of the poem, a bird seeking to free itself, brings to mind the often-evoked Mallarméan swan, trapped in ice, whose escape signifies the success or failure of the poem itself, and the poet's creative *élan*.[2] Juxtaposed with this figure of the past is a harbinger of the future, a metallic bird—the airplane—whose noise and efficiency convey the spirit of a newly mechanized age, heralded by the futurist artists. The pilot and his plane, or the poet and his poem, have been swallowed up by the great expanse of sky. The poet, creator, or voyager continuously attempts to reach the horizon, always inaccessible but a line seemingly suggestive of absolute self-definition and freedom from the alienation of this world.

As the poem continues, the idea of distance between the poet/pilot and *others* is further developed. The line, "Des milliers des milliers de très loin sont venus à ta/conquête" ("Thousands of thousands from afar have come to your/conquest" [p. 492]), may indicate a celebration of the conquest of the airplane, that is, its successful first flight. Yet in a a more negative sense, it may suggest failure, an unsuccessful takeoff, flight, or landing. The ambiguity is, however, dispelled in the next stanza where the reception awaiting the poet/pilot is one of expected failure:

> Les bras au ciel attendant ta chute
> Sinistre récompense de ton audace
> puisque tu as voulu monter si haut

> Arms in the sky awaiting your fall
> Deadly reward for your audacity
> since you wanted to climb so high

Much later on in his work, Reverdy will further develop the theme of *au-delà*, of that which he desires most ("monter si haut") being just *beyond* his reach. The above stanza recalls the flight of Icarus whose wings melted upon nearing the realm of the heretofore unexplained *beyond*, or for that matter, once again, Mallarmé in his poem "Brise marine" ("Sea Breeze"):

> Et, peut-être, les mâts, . . .
> Sont-ils de ceux qu'un vent penche sur les naufrages
> Perdus, sans mâts, sans mâts, ni fertiles îlots. . . .

> And, perhaps, the masts, . . .
> Are those which a wind bends upon the shipwrecks
> Lost, without masts, without masts, nor fertile islets. . . .

The aesthetic attempt of the poem itself, the desired fruit of the imagined Mallarméan voyage, may be shipwrecked, destroyed by ever-haunting sterility and stagnation.[3]

Juxtaposed with the allusions to Mallarmé's graceful swan and the peacefully exotic voyage of the ship, are descriptions of the strange, metallic bird which are highly indicative of the futurist climate and its reverence for speed and efficiency. As if during the course of a nightmare, the bird or plane is seen rolling in its orbit/socket of fright

("Roule dans son orbite de frayeur"). The last terms emphasize the startling innovation and artificiality of the new era, also reflected in the description of the eye or cockpit—"Oeil électrique projecteur" ("Electric projecting eye" [493]). The eye of the airplane—its cockpit and control center—now becomes the dominant figure of the passage as penetration of the twentieth century begins.

For the remainder of the poem, the themes of innovation and creative flight become more personal, referring to the poet's literary inspiration. The images of the airplane and eye do not reappear. The poet is astraddle the past and the present, a present-future in front of which he remains admiringly amazed and frightfully horrified. If the flight of the metallic bird was all a dream, was it worth it, he wonders, to have experienced such a temporal intersection: "Dans quelques heures il va falloir descendre/Et rien n'aura servi de rien" ("In a few hours I have to descend/And nothing will have served any purpose" [493]). The poet/voyager descends to the everyday world of banality where he can find no peace within himself and so, with new determination, he again departs upon his literary journey:

> Mais voilà une chambre et des livres
>
> . . . .
>
> Je suis seul au milieu de la cour
> Je vois luire mes vitres
> Et je monte
>
> But there is a room and books
>
> . . . .
>
> I am alone in the middle of the courtyard
> I see my window panes shining
> And I go up
>
> (494)

The verb *monter* ("to climb"), again evoking Mallarmé's ascent into the azure, indicates an upward direction into the realm of literary inspiration, provoking conflict among the poet's creative forces. Yet through this conflict he will come to know himself.

The initial problems encountered in poetic creation are set forth in a manner much more specific in the poem "Sujets" ("Subjects"), a piece composed more in the tone of an *art poétique*. Here the poet turns not only to the dilemma of thematic renewal but also to that of linguistic rebirth:

> Assez chanté les tours et les airs d'autrefois
> Il faut renouveler la façade des mots
> De ceux qui veulent dire et qui ne peuvent pas

> Enough sung the rounds and melodies of times past
> We must renew the façade of words
> Of those which bear meaning and of those which can not
> (499)

The facades of words, facile, artificial, and arbitrary conceal and betray true meaning; Reverdy suggests, then, that it is time to remove the primary, superficial layer of a linguistic term and to reduce it to its authentic, primitive meaning.[4] The theme of restoring true semantic density to linguistic expressions will be further discussed in some of Reverdy's later poetry and aesthetics where it is considered in greater detail.

Aside from the technical aspects of the literary craft, the problematic conventions of theme and expression, there arises the matter of the artist's attitude at the moment of inspiration as well as that of the reader during the transmission and reception of the idea:

> Mais que pense encore celui-ci
> Il ne dit rien
> Il ne sait pas parler
> Il attend le signal pour rire ou pour pleurer
> Le visage couvert la flamme qui descend
> le sang léger d'un coeur usé qui se repent

> But what does he still think
> He says nothing
> He does not know how to speak
> He awaits the signal to laugh or cry
> His face covered the flame which descends
> the light blood of a heart worn out and repentant
> (499)

The poet or reader, for the identity of the pronoun *il* is ambiguous here, is mute; he is content to await a sign—perhaps a deceptive one, arbitrary and utilitarian, such as a superficial connotation—before reacting emotionally. The covered face indicates that the poet or reader is masked and protected from, and hence, closed to, any source of innovation, whether for the purpose of writing or understanding. When the creative flame (itself a term more suggestive of poet than of reader) descends into the unknown repositories of the soul, the adjectives describing its discovery—weightless and insignificant ("le sang léger"), worn out ("d'un coeur usé"), and repentant ("qui se repent") link this passage with the preceding one. Only meaningless, overtried expressions are to be found; the creative soul is wrought with remorse. Yet the poet refuses to surrender; instead, he confronts the demands of his creative core and those of life.

More at ease at the realization that he can create, the poet achieves a more original thematic expression, as he selects an ending for his work that is also a beginning:

> J'étais seul devant le mur sans fin rebelle à mes efforts
> J'ai ouvert cette lourde porte et je n'en suis pas mort
> Debout entre les hauts portants
> Je restais immobile et regardais souvent. . . .

> I was alone in front of the endless wall rebellious to my efforts
> I opened this heavy door and I did not die of it
> Standing between the high supporters
> I remained immobile and often looked around. . . .
>
> (500)

The value of the above passage, at least for the present writer, is not so much that of a description of the emotional anxieties experienced by the successful creator, as rather a brief outline of Reverdy's future poetic expression, with its increased maturity and originality. As has already been seen in the poem "Tentative," Reverdy is preoccupied with the lack of communication and of general understanding among men. In future poems, Reverdy will treat this theme not so much in terms of an uncaring and uninterested literary audience but rather, in relation to the linear setting of the poem. Line will become one of the foremost thematic figures in Reverdy's work, a principal means of depicting human separation and hostility. In almost every volume of poetry that he wrote, there is either an emphasis on horizontal line— roads, countryside, the horizon—or on vertical line, represented especially by the wall, where motion, although sometimes permitted, is usually only minimal with limited development. The wall in the above passage is appropriately without end; it will forever provide an obstacle to successful literary creation within the poet, and without, not only in terms of artistic recognition but also in relation to basic human communication.

Linked to the figure of the wall where movement is either nonexistent or minimal, is the use of prepositions connoting confrontation and entrapment as with "devant le mur" ("in front of"), and "entre les hauts portants" ("between"), the high supporters themselves replacements for the wall. Reverdy will use several prepositions to establish linear setting, and further discussion of his development of this technique will appear below. There is no question as to the poet's immobility. His activity is reduced to remaining or taking a position ("rester") and observing ("regarder"). Indeed, in much of Reverdy's poetry written before his religious crisis, movement and human interaction are at a minimum, the narrator being content to merely observe.

In contrast to the rest of the above quoted passage is the line describing movement achieved and introducing the theme of weight: "J'ai ouvert cette lourde porte. . . ." The heavy door probably signifies an interior, intellectual obstacle, that is, the portal protecting the sacred repositories where the poet's heretofore unexplored creative impulses lie. Although formidable, the conquest of this obstacle is possible; it does not entrap or alienate men from men, as does its exterior counterpart. The theme of weight, seen here in a more positive light, is usually found to be negative in Reverdy's work. Objects accumulate and pile up, and their comprehensive weight usually prohibits passage, in short, they are often reflections of the wall.[5]

In addition to "Sujets," another poem from *Cale sèche*, "Bande de souvenirs" ("Band of Memories") develops several themes which were introduced in "Tentative" and which will consistently reappear throughout Reverdy's work, although from time to time in different forms and degrees of intensity. The theme of passage from one sphere of reality to another, treated in "Tentative" as an exterior flight from the banality of the everyday world in order to seek a superior intellectual and artistic potential, is presented in "Bande de souvenirs" as an interior descent into the poet's/voyager's subconscious in order to define his self's inner being. Briefly mentioned in "Tentative," the figure of the room serves as a vehicle for this type of passage and is usually found, as in this example, in a psychological context. The poem begins with a description of a statue, that of Mary Magdalene, which is located "Dans la chapelle au bord des routes" ("In the chapel at the edge of the roads," [469]), a site providing further reference to Reverdy's use of the horizontal line as a means of orientation and structure. The chapel along the road changes to a place of refuge in the mind, the inner sanctuaries which are reflected in the folds of Mary Magdalene's dress:[6] "Sa robe en plâtre fait des plis/aux replis que l'âme redoute" ("Her dress of plaster makes folds/in the recesses which the soul fears"). Reverdy superimposes, here, a psychological view or *paysage* ("countryside") upon a physical view, a technique reminiscent of cubist tradition. The soul must confront the interior *paysage*, reassess its hidden values and convictions ("plis"), lying protected in its inner recesses ("replis"), for failure to do so may paralyze the intellectual faculties of the mind.

When passage has occurred through the folds of material to the inner chambers of the mind, the reader discovers a crossroads, an interior crossroads, "En deux branches le ciel bifurque" ("Into two branches the sky divides" [470]). The expression "deux branches" may indicate the two strata of existence between which the poet vacillates— the quotidian as well as the ethereally intellectual.[7] As a poetic figure the crossroads suggests that nothing has yet been resolved; that which lies within the inner sanctuaries of the soul has not yet been confronted. As the descent into the subconscious takes place, the poet must digest the material to which he is exposed, and decide what to retain or eliminate:[8] "Pour en éparpiller les plumes/forge ton envie sur l'enclume" ("In order to scatter the feathers/forge your desire on the anvil" [470]). When a decision has been reached as to which emotional fibers will be receptive to additional growth and development, the traces or remains of the material ("les plumes")[9] hidden in the inner sanctuary will be scattered and the poet will have at last confronted himself.

As soon as decisions have been made concerning the poet's artistic orientation, all conflict and discord reach a state of resolution.[10] Harmony is achieved as the journey through the mind is transformed into a voyage at sea during which the waves become agents of artistic transformation. The water effecting transition cleanses the poet through the action of the verb *mousser*. Any preconceived or socially imposed notions he may harbor are washed away, as he slips toward an authentic poetic text.[11] Besides transition, water also signifies purity and transparency—thus the authenticity of the poetic communication. The transition itself from initial inspiration to fruition occurs as "La pierre glisse/Sous ton pied nu" ("The stone slips/Under your bare foot" [470]), the adjective *nu* again confirming the state of *tabula rasa*, the creative soul laid bare, completely receptive to inspiration. The poet is rocked and transformed by the motion of the waves, which, ultimately, leave behind the waste material from the birth, "l'odorant sillage des pins" ("the odorous wake of the pines"). The traces of the birth, emitted as the ship's wake, do not actually constitute refuse, since such creative elements may be indicative of future directions in which the poet's attempts may be oriented.

Yet in spite of the constructive transformation achieved, the poet is not completely confident with regard to the future. At the end of the poem, the waves, the medium of change, have vanished; the journey has come to an abrupt end. The boat lies deserted: "Mais le navire reste en rade" ("But the ship remains layed up" [472]). Having returned from his interior voyage, the poet finds himself immobile, surrounded by the illumination of commonplace existence.

Immobility, suggested in aborted flight ("Tentative"), in confrontation with the wall ("Sujets"), and now, in the stillness of the deserted boat ("Bande de souvenirs") seems quite appropriate in view of the title *Cale sèche*. After having achieved an initial success recorded in this trilogy of poems, the mind of the poet together with its inner sanctuaries lies barren; the traces of the creative process have been erased, and there is no reason to believe that it may recur. Yet, the reader, despite Reverdy's pessimism, knows differently, for he has seen the legacy left by Reverdy, who at this point was perhaps unaware of his own capabilities.

B.   *Early Aspects of Space and Temporality in the Voyage*

A principal theme in Reverdy's work, the voyage is inscribed in an aesthetic context, as discussed above, as well as in a metaphysical context, evolving progressively from the simple, solitary voyager traveling to escape the well-defined limits of his past to, finally, a figure of human alienation, seeking to escape the Pascalian notion that life has been reduced to the status of jetsam, matter haphazardly tossed into a meaningless world. While the theme of the voyage is treated in a more positive light in Reverdy's earlier poetry, it will be seen, in later texts, to bear a negative connotation. The relevant poems offered as testimony to the preponderance of this theme throughout Reverdy's work will, like those of the previously discussed trilogy, show varying degrees of originality, some borrowing heavily from nineteenth-century poetry, others being quite original.

A voyage from the present to the past and then onward to the future is depicted in yet another poem from *Cale sèche*, "Départ" ("Departure"), a title evoking the poetry of Baudelaire and Mallarmé. The narrator, attempting to flee a present of stagnation, finds that the past is now only a memory, an accumulation of incidents which, although weighty, are paradoxically empty, meaningless: "Une grande chambre pleine de visages qui passent/et tournent tournent encore" ("A large room full of faces which are passing/and are turning still turning" [505]). The figure of the room (here used differently than in its context of privileged repository as in the poem "Bande de souvenirs") signifies past accumulation, a filled space, yet, at the same time, a void. There is no order among the past incidents, the verbs *passer* suggesting continuous movement and *tourner* indicating uncontrolled direction. Since the narrator will find no sense or meaning in such a journey, he looks to future movement as an outlet for the frustration of his present: "La saison revient je pars pour toujours" ("The season returns I am leaving forever" [505]).

The optimistic view of a journey into the future is somewhat diminished in the poem "Passant" ("Passing" or "A Passer-by"), again from *Cale sèche*. It begins with a tone of levity, but ends on a more serious note. "Passant" is more original than "Départ," emphasizing human alienation as opposed to aesthetic dissatisfaction and *malaise*. As in the beginning of the poem "Tentative," the voyage is to be made along the horizontal line, at the same time a profile of the physical terrain and a blueprint of a human life. Seeking change in order to avoid the status quo, the narrator is attracted to this transformative space. However, as the horizon appears in more detail, it becomes "Un long ruban de camelote" ("A long ribbon of cheap trash" [455]); hope for change grows faint. The earlier cyclical order and restraint in nature have vanished, leaving behind a countryside seen as entanglement or complication ("paysages embrouillés" ["entangled countrysides"]). Each point along the line of confusion symbolizes an act of hostility on the part of the environment: "Sur l'un ou l'autre que je saute/Mon Dieu mes souliers sont percés" ("On one or the other where I jump/My God my shoes are broken through").

The voyage, as Reverdy visualizes it in *Cale sèche*, is also seen as an ineluctable journey into death. The tone of the poet's lugubrious chant varies, ironically sometimes humorous as in Baudelaire's *badinage* with death, sometimes spectral and glacial, doleful, yet resigned and passive. The poem "Au Saut du rêve" ("On Getting Out of the Dream"), testifies to this mood of doleful resignation, as the poet relives a nightmare, specifically, his own funeral ceremony, subsequent cortege, and burial. Described in the first person throughout, and, therefore, with an appeal more individual to the reader, the poem, as evident in other texts, is based on the theme of line: first, the script of the ceremony itself, then, the procession to the cemetery. A supporting theme to that of the ultimate, linear journey is the substance of finite space, that is, the weight and thickness of death itself.

At the poem's outset, line and weight, temporality and space are immediately linked: "J'assistais à la cérémonie/Et très péniblement je supportais l'idée de ma mort" ("I was present at the ceremony/And very painfully I bore the idea of my death" [484]). The verb *supporter* suggests tolerating or bearing a burden. Another allusion to space is revealed in a further line where the presence of weight is more specific: " . . . la plus grande peine à soulever ce poids" (" . . . the greatest pain to lift this weight")—the cadaver. Besides weight, the space of death has a certain thickness, suggested in the following line, "On dirait même qu'il faut mâcher cette épaisseur" ("One would even say that one has to chew this thickness" [484]).

As an additional support to the linear theme of the funeral script, to the notion of spatial substance, the poet attempts to reconstruct, through memory, the principal lines of his face. The temporal aid of memory fails the poet, and it is once more the notion of space which realizes the linear setting, the cortege itself; space and line unite to lend reality to the modicum of existence the voyager possesses—his own death procession:

> Enfin nous redescendîmes dans la rue
> Cortège expiatoire
> Personne n'attendait
> Je m'acheminai seul vers le mystère que j'allais enfin connaître
> . . . .
> Une à une je voyais revenir mes mauvaises actions
> La terre était ouverte au repentir

> Finally we again descended into the street
> Expiatory cortege
> No one was waiting
> I proceeded alone toward the mystery that I was at last going to know
> . . . .

> One by one I saw coming back my bad deeds
> The earth was open to repentance
>
> (485)

Besides the weight and thickness comes the solitude; the poet/voyager makes the last steps of the journey alone. The reader can only wonder about the term *cortege*—it may perhaps suggest only the preacher and those who bear the coffin, no relatives, no friends, no one else. The horror of death, of what the voyager may be about to suffer, causes him to reflect upon his past, and this time, memory, again seen spatially as accumulation, stores of events, aids him to repent. The situation of the poet haunted by the idea that he may deserve his punishment because of past actions again brings to mind a poem of Baudelaire, "Un Voyage à Cythère," ("A Voyage to Cytherea"), also from *Les Fleurs du mal,* in which the poet also repents, seeing himself as the gallows victim.[12]

Death, during the course of Reverdy's poem, does not come, for the poet, as indicated in the title, awakens from his dream. Resigned to the solitary journey, the voyage into finitude in time and space, the poet confides to the reader, in a most confidential and personal couplet, that human hope is only an illusion: "Tandis que monte au loin cette lente rengaine/L'or du soleil crevé coule et son flot nous mène" ("While there rises in the distance this slow, old refrain/The gold of the burst sun runs out and its flow leads us" [485]). The gold particles constitute human expectation, all positive aspects of life, which, once the solar disk ruptures, will flow out into the void that is actuality. The theme of rupture recalls the breach in the wall from "Bande de souvenirs"— a breach which opens or flows into emptiness. Penetration of the wall is meaningless, as are the shreds of hope, the traces of gold particles to which humanity looks for orientation.

This first attempt to create poetry can be viewed, then, as a glimpse of what the future years will bring to Reverdy's craft. As an artist, and perhaps as a person, Reverdy was pessimistic and joyless, and his work bears out this testimony. Yet, he left behind so much more than just his moments of unhappiness. What is important to perceive is the very substance of his poetry, not simply its cosmetic appearance. Such a task is probably an impossible accomplishment, whence arises its appeal.

II   Poèmes en prose *and* Quelques poèmes

Poèmes en prose (Prose Poems) and *Quelques poèmes (Several Poems)* reflect specifically several literary trends prevalent during Rev-

erdy's early years in Paris to which *Cale sèche* refers only generally in
such poems as "Tentative" and "Sujets." Sources of influence such as
cubism and futurism dictate the structure and setting of several poems
in both *Poèmes en prose* and in *Quelques poèmes*. In addition, both
collections contain poems about World War I, but frequently, especially in *Poèmes en prose*, the war is used simply as background. The
better war poems are to be found in *Quelques poèmes* where they
serve as bitter protests against self-wrought destruction.

Poèmes en prose,[13] Reverdy's first attempt to write poetry in prose,
continues the themes of a basic lack of human communication, both
for the artist and for his fellowmen, as well as that of the voyage, which
here, in this collection, assumes a different shape—that of a circle—a
voyage that in a sense never began, movement experienced as non-
movement. Besides the circular line, the spiral is introduced, together
with the already familiar horizontal and vertical lines. However, in this
collection it is the intersection of the horizontal and vertical which is
especially stressed, that is, its capacity to paralyze and imprison. In
contrast to the noticeable absence of punctuation in *Cale sèche*, Reverdy reverts to traditional punctuation in his first volume of prose
poems but later abandons it for the most part in *Quelques poèmes*.

A.   The Testament of Cubism and Futurism

Many of Reverdy's early poems may have been inspired by a glance
at a painting by Braque, Picasso, or Gris, but in the case of the text
"Saltimbanques" ("Tumblers") from *Poèmes en prose*, the evidence
points overwhelmingly to Picasso. In this two-paragraph poem, a very
simple scene is described in terms of noticeable economy: there are
two anonymous figures, a child and a man who dance and lift weights
in the middle of a mob, equally anonymous. The futility of the per-
formance is marked by the terms "force inutile" ("useless strength"
[52]). Clothed in a garment much too large for him, the child holds out
a purse to the crowd—but in vain. Although surrounded by a multitude, the circus figures stand alone with only their poverty. What
comes to mind with this poem are Picasso's numerous tableaux from
his "rose period" (1904–1906) which abound with tragic adolescents
from the carnival milieu he observed as he frequented the Medrano
circus.[14]

The painter whose tableau may have inspired the text "Les Poètes"
("The Poets") is unknown, but the source is most likely cubist. A more

or less static description of one or possibly two figures structured upon superimposed planes is then juxtaposed with spiral movement which is ultimately neutralized. The scene begins at the position of a lamp and the oval brightness of its shade. Except for the circular movement which is inherent in the linguistic location *autour de* ("around")—the roundness of the lampshade which encircles the objects and the figure(s) of the poem, the description is otherwise static. Moreover, the circular line of the lampshade connotes protection and shelter: "Sa tête s'abritait craintivement sous l'abat-jour de la lampe" ("His head apprehensively took shelter under the lampshade" [34]). As for the figure(s), there is surely one—a musician who does not stir and possibly another, reflected in the possessive adjective *sa* in the terms "sa tête." Although the musician is described as sleeping, his hands are supposedly playing the violin: "Il dort; ses mains coupées jouent du violon pour lui faire oublier sa misère" ("He sleeps; his severed hands play the violin to make him forget his misery"). It is possible that in this first paragraph there are three superimposed planes of reality: first, the head of a poet, of the musician, or of another artist at the lamp; second, the sleeping musician; third, the subconscious wandering of the musician as he perhaps dreams he is playing his instrument. The past participle *coupées* indicates that there is no question of a scene from conventional reality; what matters here is not the subjects themselves, but the text or tableau as a whole, and the separated hands which play the violin provide another dimension of reality, enhancing the autonomy of the poem as an entirety, the poem as an object.

Rupture and superimposition also dictate the structure of a 1914 painting by Braque, *Femme à la guitare* (*Woman with a Guitar*)[15] in which the upper part of the woman's body is completely dissociated from the lower part. Overlapping geometric planes present multiple views of her head and shoulders, whereas her hands, which hold the guitar, appear at the bottom of the tableau, almost concealed by layers of music sheets, newspapers, and several angles of the instrument itself. Both the poem and this painting represent a collection of several appearances of a subject fused into a single image.[16]

Returning to the poem itself, the reader must consider the presence of immobility in more than just cubist terms, more than the result of multiple views, the destruction of experiential or existential context. Immobility is also indicative of the artist's(s') dejected state. The lack of artistic activity—the separation of mind from hands—would seem to suggest a stagnant mind, barren of inspiration. Moreover, the circular line of the lampshade may well allude to their unproductivity, reflecting the artistic voids which they have become. The medium of prose as opposed to the free verse of *Cale sèche* increases the effect of immobile space, seen here as intellectual paralysis.

Movement starts at the beginning of the second paragraph, appearing as a series of half-completed circles, or more precisely, spirals: "Un escalier qui ne conduit nulle part grimpe autour de la maison" ("A stairway which leads nowhere climbs around the house" [34]). Here the verb *grimper* suggests the act of climbing *around* in a slow, deliberate manner, similar to the motion of one drawing a clear, precise line. The absence of openings in the building diminishes the sense of context the paragraph does have, that is, the location of the house. In addition, it contributes a feeling of imprisonment or paralysis to the position *autour de*—if the poem has a conventional context at all, it is a linguistic one, with the few objects and figures existing in terms of being located *around* the lampshade and stairway.

As the circular movement continues, the spirals are traced by hasty, abrupt gestures. However, the cyclical motion *around,* which they connote, remains unfruitful, since the shadows have fallen under the same malevolent spell as have the unproductive artists: " . . . le musicien qui joue toujours du violon avec ses mains qui ne l'écoutent pas" (" . . . the musician who is still playing the violin with his hands that are not listening to him"). These last lines of the poem serve as the only link between the two paragraphs—between the static, cubist tableau of the beginning, and the anecdotal, spirited but aimless scene at the end. Each spiral will continue to pass *around* its predecessor, retracing the imprisoning climb *around* a space barren of all artistic stimulation. Movement has, in effect, been neutralized.

Reverdy's interest in the static art of cubism, in the exclusion of existential or experiential context, is manifested in a slightly different type of prose poem from the volume *Quelques poèmes,*[17] published just one year after *Poèmes en prose.* The technique of collage (a pasting together, literally), practiced by Picasso, Braque, and Gris among others, can be observed in a series of eight unrelated prose poems entitled "Carrés" ("Squares"). A collage in cubist terms is a tableau in which bits of commonplace objects, newspapers, cloth, music sheets, etc. are pasted together, incongruously and arbitrarily for their suggestive effect, in a sense a more realistic rendition of the superimposition of painted planes.[18] Arranged on two consecutive pages, the shapes of the poems in "Carrés" form a tableau; it is not the individual poem which prevails, but instead, the effect of the collective perimeters:

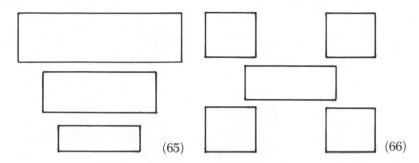

To take just one of these poems as an example of static art, let the reader consider the following text in which a mask is presented in an environment isolated from other related subjects and suspended in time:

> Les cheveux coupés, la
> tête tranchée, le sabre
> restait encore entre ses
> dents. Le bourreau ama-
> teur pleurait et sa figure
> était un masque. On
> l'avait importé de Chine
> et il ne savait plus être
> cruel.

> The hair shorn, the
> head severed, the saber
> still remained between his
> teeth. The amateur executioner
> was crying and his face
> was a mask. They had
> imported it from China
> and he no longer knew how to be
> cruel.

(66)

In contrast to the poems of cubist origin which emphasize the immobile and static states of people and objects, is a text, probably of futurist inspiration, entitled "Le Patineur céleste" ("The Celestial Skater"), from the collection *Poèmes en prose*. The futurists, although sharing certain points of view with the cubists—such as the multiplicity of view in order to simultaneously depict numerous sensations in

time, decomposition and dismemberment of objects, superimposition
of surfaces—opposed the cubists' preoccupation with immobility;
instead, the futurists preferred and affirmed the dynamism of the modern world, the plastic value of movement,[19] both of which they exalted
in their glorification of the machine, of the mechanized, commercial
object.[20]

Passage along a sidewalk is suddenly accelerated in the poem "Le
Patineur céleste" as human life is transformed into a swift journey,
permitting no time for reflection or analysis, as the sidewalk abruptly
becomes a skating rink where a race is taking place. The narration of
the event is based upon a double superimposition. The skater, identified by the title of the poem, is paradoxically seen by the narrator as
a cyclist: "On ne voit pas ses mains et le guidon remplace les pédales"
("One does not see his hands and the handlebars replace the pedals"
[37]). The description of the skater's movements, gliding one into the
other, brings to mind a futurist tableau of 1912 by Marcel Duchamp,
Nu descendant l'escalier (*Nude Descending the Staircase*).[21] It is easy
to imagine several pedal positions, each superimposed upon the other
in quick succession, as in the abrupt, fragmented descent of
Duchamp's figure. Another possible interpretation is that the position
and movements of the hands and feet form one unified action, reveal-
ing only a blurred image of the wheel as it spins around faster and
faster.

The term "futurist" as applied to Duchamp in this particular painting, as well as to Reverdy in this text, must, however, be used with
caution. John Golding in his *Le Cubisme* (*Cubism*) calls Duchamp's
tableau an illustration of a passage from the *Futurist Manifesto*. Yet
Golding tempers his judgment by adding that Duchamp's painting is
only futurist in the intense movement of its overlapping planes, anti-
futurist in its cynical satire of a civilization obsessed with mechanized
objects, and moreover, in its depiction of a nude, the representation of
which had been ordered suppressed by the *Manifesto*.[22] Similarly, it
is quite possible that Reverdy has selected an apparently futurist scene
for the purpose of interpreting it in a negative mode. Although action
occurs, it is then reversed, producing a zero count and rendering the
movement completely ineffective. In spite of the rapid, spinning movement, the skater does not progress; he is instead changed into fixated
motion. As he passes in front of a mirror, the movement of his limbs
is captured visually and in a sense he is paralyzed. The image regis-

tered by the mirror cannot be altered unless the skater passes again. It is at the mirror that immobility and mobility intersect; movement recorded at its highest speed is simultaneously realized and negated, its recorded fragment being reduced to permanence, to mobile fixation. Perhaps, after all, the possibility of dynamic movement is only an illusion, and the enthusiasm of the newly mechanized age, a silly whim.

B. Interior Disorder: Aimless Movement and Linear Imprisonment

Other examples of senseless journeys and aimless movement abound in the collection *Poèmes en prose*. As a principal theme, the voyage undertaken seeks its independence from the tradition of Baudelaire, Mallarmé, and Rimbaud, and even the cubists and futurists. Although indissolubly linked to the past, these poems abandon the aesthetic objective and now stress the lack of meaning that the journey represents to the voyager who has departed for the express purpose of restoring meaning to his life.[23]

In another poem entitled "Voyages trop grands" ("Voyages Too Great"), the simultaneity of the exterior setting (both a linear and circular itinerary) gives the impression that in spite of the intense speed of the train, the traveler has not moved. His view from the train is described as " . . . le paysage qui allait, à rebours . . ." (" . . . the countryside which was going backward . . ." [48]). The passenger is disoriented, for as he slips backward along the route, the train races forward. Confronted with the senselessness of reality, he remains spellbound: "De son rôle, qu'il jouait avec le plus grand sérieux, il lui manquait la signification" ("Of his role, which he played most seriously, he lacked the significance").

True self-identity has not been realized; reality here seems to be a series of appearances or masquerades. The futility of the horizontal route now becomes apparent as the traveler returns to the very point from which he departed. It is with sarcasm that the poet speaks of "sa tâche bien remplie" ("his task well carried out"), for several lines earlier he confided to us that "Sa tête doit rester vide et rien ne pourrait la remplir" ("His head must remain empty and nothing could fill it"). Departed, yet never really having left, fulfilling a responsibility but still leaving it void—such is the dilemma of Reverdy's voyager: "On arrivera, on repartira éternellement sur les routes toujours les mêmes malgré leur nombre" ("You will arrive, you will eternally leave again

upon routes always the same in spite of their number" [36]). Such is
the conclusion from another poem of aimless wandering, "Salle
d'attente" ("Waiting Room"), also from *Poèmes en prose*.

In addition to bearing a more original interpretation of the voyage,
the collection *Poèmes en prose* also emphasizes what has now become
one of Reverdy's principal preoccupations—the figure of line. The horizontal lines of the poems from *Cale sèche*, all generally indicative of
wayfaring and ironical horizontality—sidewalk ("trottoir"), path
("sentier, allée, chemin"), corridor ("couloir"), procession ("cortège"),
rivers and riverbanks ("ruisseaux, rives"), borders of objects
("bords")—merge with the vertical lines, spirals, and circles which
begin to appear in *Poèmes en prose* and continue throughout much of
Reverdy's poetry. It is not simply the use of linear figures which makes
Reverdy's preoccupation apparent, but rather, his own admission of
the interior disorder he is experiencing: " . . . mais dans la ville où le
dessin nous *emprisonne, l'arc de cercle* du porche, les *carrès* des
fenêtres, les *losanges* des *toits*. . . . Dans ma tête des *lignes*, rien que
des *lignes;* si je pouvais y mettre un peu d'ordre seulement" (" . . . but
in the town where *pattern emprisons* us, the *arc of the circle* of the
porch, the *squares* of the *windows*, the *diamond shapes* of the *roofs*
. . . . *Lines* in my head, nothing but lines; if I could only put them in
order").[24]

The threat of linear emprisonment with which Reverdy is so often
obsessed, is frequently suggested by the figure of the wall, inherently
connotative of the human separation and hostility stressed throughout
his work. Similar to the static poems of cubist inspiration, those in
which the wall as a setting is particularly emphasized reveal only minimal motion. Determination to find a means through the wall or barrier
is frequently replaced by a resigned, taciturn acceptance; the disappearance of one principal barrier only assures that others will appear
in succession to take its place. One such example is provided in a poem
from *Poèmes en prose*, "L'Esprit sort" ("The Mind Leaves"),[25] the title
of which implies freedom of passage. However, the free association of
ideas suggested in the title is promptly negated by the composition of
the library walls. Reinforced by fixed layers of intellectual material,
the walls are formed by intersecting lines of numerous flat, rectangular
surfaces. Beginning as small versions of restricting lines, the books will
multiply until their numbers join to construct the partitions of the
library.[26]

In addition to the wall, another illustration of linear enclosure is
found in poems where the setting is especially linguistic in nature, a

device which I have characterized as "linguistic location" in another study.[27] A linguistic location is created by using prepositional phrases which suggest arrangements of abstract horizontal and vertical lines. It is a setting defined solely in the position denoted by its respective prepositions. The previously discussed poem "Les Poètes" (in *Poèmes en prose*) is an example of such a location; the circular movement of light *around* the oval lampshade encircles the room and its occupants, offering them protection, but also imprisoning them in an artistic void. Then the circle is replaced by the spiral, as the stairway, appearing in the form of half-completed circles or spirals, climbs *around* the house, sequestering those inside. Shadows along the stairway trace the spirals, climb to the top, fall, begin to rise anew—but all for naught—the stairway leads nowhere; there are not even doors or windows. The movement *around* results in only encirclement, cyclical sterility, and stagnation. Although there is no one specific setting in the poem "O" from *Quelques poèmes*, there is an emphasis upon the observer, what he sees, and his position *on* the sidewalk: "Je serai là encore demain matin/Sur le trottoir" ("I will still be there tomorrow morning/On the sidewalk" [68]). As the elements of the *collage* pass by, overlap, fade, reappear, the only definite, stable element of the text is the observer who *is*, *exists* (his being reinforced by his position *on*), yet, who, during the course of the poem, never *becomes*.

Cessation of movement once begun is conveyed in the preposition "between" in the texts "Le Vent et l'esprit" ("Wind and Mind") and "Des Êtres vagues" ("Vague Beings"), both from *Poèmes en prose*. In the former poem, a phantasmal head places itself *between* two iron supports: "La tête, . . . se place entre les deux fils de fer et se cale et se tient; rien ne bouge" ("The head, . . . places itself *between* two iron wires and wedges itself and affixes itself; nothing moves" [29]). The motion of placement *between* is counterbalanced by the cessation of this movement, confirmed by the expression *se tenir*. The location of the head is now absolutely fixed. Although interaction with it is repeatedly attempted by a personnage referred to as "je" ("I"), the immobility inherent in the position *entre* negates any effect the words uttered by the head may have.

Elsewhere, in another text, "Des Êtres vagues," it is the poet himself who has initially been caught *between*—waiting for some meaningful element to befall him in his solitude, and confronting the senselessness of the natural world: "A présent je passe *entre* les deux trottoirs; je suis seul, avec le vent qui m'accompagne en se moquant de moi. Comment fuir ailleurs que dans la nuit" ("At present I pass *between* the two sidewalks; I am alone, with the wind which accompanies me, while making fun of me. How to flee elsewhere than into the night" [45; italics mine]). However, in spite of the abject discouragement of the scene, the poet sees that there is still one more place to flee—into the poem: "Mais la table et la lampe sont là qui m'attendent . . ." ("But the table and the lamp are there which await me . . ."). Art, poetry, and the word constitute refuges from the absurdity that is reality, and will satisfy, at least in this poem, the poet's state of *attente*, wating for meaning, for creative inspiration.

III   La Lucarne ovale

Unlike the three preceding collections of poetry, *La Lucarne ovale* (*The Oval Garret Window*)[28] contains several very brief poems, such as the following, which are extremely autobiographical, testifying to the hardships of Reverdy's early years in Paris:

> Quand la lampe n'est pas encore éteinte,
> quand le feu commence à pâlir et que le
> soleil se cache, il y a quand même dans la
> rue des gens qui passent.

> When the lamp is not yet extinguished, when
> the fire begins to grow dim and the sun lies
> in hiding, even so there are people in the
> street who pass by.
>
> (89)

Published in 1916, this collection recalls the time when Reverdy was living in a dormer room (hence the title) from which he would gaze out and record what he saw:

> En ce temps-là le charbon était devenu aussi
> précieux et rare que des pépites d'or et
> j'écrivais dans un grenier où la neige, en
> tombant par les fentes du toit, devenait bleue.

> At that time coal had become as precious and
> rare as gold nuggets and I was writing in a
> garret room where the snow, while falling by
> the cracks in the roof, took on a blue tinge.
>
> (75)

Later, in *Le Gant de crin,* a work of aesthetics, Reverdy will return to the image of gold nuggets, precious components of literary inspiration. One other expression from this poem is particularly significant, the term *fentes* ("cracks")—the themes of splitting, decomposition, and deterioration will become progressively more important in Reverdy's poetry, until as in his last works particularly, all motion is of a destructive nature. It is especially in *La Lucarne ovale* that he begins to emphasize the theme of the *trou* or hole, a theme which anticipates his later poems of rupture and disunity.

A. *Transiency and Separation*

The hole, abyss, or void become linked to the previously discussed figure of the wall; the sides of the hole or the lines inscribing the void impose walls or restricting partitions. The barriers and enclosures they form continue to appear throughout *La Lucarne ovale,* and will remain fundamental figures in Reverdy's work. In another autobiographical text of simple beauty he sees the wall in a surprisingly favorable light, for it can be climbed; the figure of the barrier is then combined with that of the *trou* or hole, which also surprisingly appears in a positive context—*la lucarne:*

> Aux premières lueurs du jour je me suis levé
> lentement. Je suis monté à l'échelle du mur et,
> par la lucarne, j'ai regardé passer les gens qui
> s'en allaient.
>
> At the first glimmers of day I slowly got up.
> I climbed up the wall and by the garret window,
> I watched the people pass by who were
> departing.
>
> (102)

The garret window represents some small measure of freedom for the poet who from this vantage point returns in countless poems to the ever-constant refrain—"les gens qui passaient, qui s'en allaient."

Driven by the need to end his solitude and meaninglessness, Reverdy and his traveler or narrator constantly push onward in order to relate to those who are impassively drifting. One fundamental difference in the treatment of the theme of the voyage in *La Lucarne ovale* is the emphasis upon the *je;* Reverdy places himself at the center, instead of

an impersonal *on* or an unknown traveler. The same emphasis is present in other themes throughout the collection—suddenly the poet confronts his own problems directly and accepts them as part of his identity. In one final example of his autobiographical narration, "D'Un
autre ciel" ("From Another Sky"), a poem of irregular rhyme without
punctuation (as are most of the poems of *La Lucarne ovale*), Reverdy
identifies himself with all lonely travelers who long for their home-
towns. Disappointed by what they had expected to find, proceeding
from one station to another, they change trains and sadly watch those
voyagers who are being met, certain they will find no one awaiting
them. Upon arriving, in this particular text, the voyager is met only by
the noise of the train and the din and confusion of the station. There
is no one to welcome him.

B.   *Motion Increased: The Whirlwind and Figures of Rupture*

Indeed, the efficacy of the voyage as a vehicle for self-definition and
inner acceptance is weighed in a text entitled "Droit vers la mort"
("Straight Toward Death") in which the poet questions his previous
trust in wayfaring. The departures and arrivals of crammed trains are
described as "télégrammes éplorés" ("tearful telegrams"); their mes-
sage will serve no purpose, but merely indicates imminent failure. In
spite of reserved hope, the poet realizes that the outcome of the voyage
is an assumed risk, a wager that the uncertainty inscribed along the
circular itinerary—its shape being the only certainty—will eventually
lend meaningfulness to the destination:

> Il faut passer un espace infernal
> Risquer plus que l'on n'a
> Et partir revenir s'en aller
>
> It is necessary to pass through a diabolical space
> Risk more than one has
> And leave come back go away again
>
>   (77)

By this time, the traveler has hardened from his aimless wayfaring—
"Plus de larmes enfin dans un coeur desséché" ("Finally no more tears
in a heart gone dry" [78]). Retaining no hope, the voyager passively
accepts his end which, in this poem, is foreshadowed by the appearance of the whirlwind and followed by his collapse, perhaps caused by
the whirlwind, perhaps initiated by some unknown force:

—Un tourbillon l'a pris—

Et lorsque dans la nuit il tomba pour jamais

Personne n'entendit le nom qu'il prononçait

—A whirlwind took him—

And when in the night he fell forever
No one heard the name that he pronounced

The figure of the whirlwind which is closely associated here with destructive motion downward, is elsewhere in Reverdy's poetry, as the reader will see, synonymous with violent, abusive, circular motion; confusing contortions will distort and eventually create rupture. The position of this figure, the first indicating a violent, uncontrolled event, is significant. By placing the phrase "—Un tourbillon l'a pris—" to the middle of those which precede and follow, Reverdy breaks the slow rhythm of the previous lines as the decision to continue is weighed, and lends added emphasis to the following lines which describe the end already anticipated in the title "Droit vers la mort." It is in *La Lucarne ovale* especially that Reverdy begins to take liberty with the left margin, occasionally varying the point at which it begins to add such emphasis. In later works this technique, which one critic[29] has called "visual verse," will assume an even more important role. One other aspect of the ending of this poem should be pointed out—as the traveler falls to his death, he utters a name that no one hears: to his physical demise there is the added dimension of his spiritual-verbal demise, and for that matter, an aesthetic death—that of the text itself. The voyager has disappeared, and because his identity has not been learned, the poet cannot continue; the text appropriately fades. The reader will soon discover that the transitory quality of Reverdy's poetry—the text's fragility and its frequent disappearance—will intensify, becoming an integral component of his later style.

The forever circular itinerary of the voyage is viewed from yet another angle in the poem "Les Vides du printemps" ("The Voids of Spring"). Here, the season of spring, usually connoting a positive rebirth or renewal, accentuates all the more the cyclical sterility of the journey undertaken. Dominating the entire poem is the theme of the *vide* ("void" or "vacuum"), sometimes seen as a hole into which the path disappears, the encirclement formed by hostile walls and streets, and finally the mirror into which the poet gazes in search of an answer to the impasse—imprisonment within a sterile cycle, the neutrality of the traveler's position. He has departed but never arrived; he has arrived but never left.

Again, the poem begins with downward motion, "En passant une seule fois devant ce trou j'ai penché/mon front" ("While once passing in front of this hole I bent/down" [79]). Death or perhaps simply a mirror reflecting the traveler's long-sought identity—such are the possibilities indicated by the pit and confirmed by the four succeeding lines, all of which repeatedly emphasize the notion of an interrogation or a quest:

> Qui est là
> Quel chemin est venu finir à cet endroit
> Quelle vie arrêtée
> Que je ne connais pas
>
> Who is there
> What road has come to end at this place
> What a halted life
> Which I do not know

(79)

As the traveler attempts to gain a clear vision of what the pit may mean, an observation is made of that which is occurring around him: "Et quelqu'un vient le long du mur/On le poursuit" ("And someone is coming along the wall/They are pursuing him"). Who is the "quelqu'un," the "On"—as usual, there is no answer. With the exception of the traveler, narrator, or poet, those who appear in Reverdy's poetry are anonymous; having no precise identity, they merely represent an impersonal mass.

The theme of pursuit, previously expressed in the third person, now changes to the first-person singular. Whether the narrator is actually the "quelqu'un" pursued, or whether he has just watched him, the narrator takes flight, driven onward by his fear of the pit. Wherever he turns, he experiences encircling lines and enclosure. The deserted, unwelcoming streets evoke Chirico's lonely urban scenes:

> Les rues désertes tournent
> Les maisons sont fermées
> Je ne peux plus sortir
> Et personne pourtant ne m'avait enfermé

The deserted streets twist
The houses are closed
I can no longer go out
And yet no one had shut me in

(79)

Although there is curiously no sign of human presence, a deadly force is at play, indicated by the verb *tourner* ("to turn," "to twist"), whose twisting motion recalls the lethal whirlwind in the text "Droit vers la mort." However, the contortions of Reverdy's streets distinguish this scene from those of Chirico where all movement is suppressed.

Later in the poem, when the presence of *others* is introduced, it is a hostile one. The traveler learns to rely exclusively upon himself; there is no one from whom he may seek directions. Yet, despite his efforts, he cannot escape the pit: "Puis le trou s'est rouvert/Toujours le même/ Toujours aussi transparent/Et toujours aussi clair." ("Then the hole reopened/Always the same/Always as transparent/And always as clear" [80]. Now, when aperture is finally realized, it is negative. The repetition of the adverb "toujours," recalling the succession of the interrogative pronouns at the beginning, is used ironically; its transparence or clarity restricts, having previously given no precise meaning. However, when the poem has come full circle and the poet is again confronted with the pit, it now appears to him as a mirror reflecting a familiar face—his own; he and his efforts, the voyage, his life—all are part of the void and there will be no escape: "Autrefois j'avais regardé ce miroir vide et n'y avais rien vu/Du visage oublié à présent reconnu" ("I had formerly looked into this empty mirror and had seen nothing there / Of the forgotten face presently recognized").

The theme of closure, whether seen in a psychological sense—hostility or indifference—or in a physical sense—barred doors, streets, and houses—will become associated in *La Lucarne ovale* with a greater degree of movement, for the most part destructive. The lightness and gaiety suggested in the title of the prose poem "Joies d'été" ("Joys of Summer") are only superficial features, soon dispelled by the quickening rhythm of dancers propelled by a vicious whirlwind. The movements of the crowd which has gathered to dance at this summer celebration are described by the verb *tourner* and are limited by combinations of surrounding lines and barriers. The twisting motion of their bodies as they seek to avoid such obstacles approximates the shape of the whirlwind itself. As the dancers move faster, so does the natural

background of the tableau, until all participating elements are trapped
in an intense rapidity:

> Le bal est un tourbillon, et le vent sort pour
> secouer les branches qui tremblent. . . . La terre
> s'évapore en poussière et vole. . . .

> The ball is a whirlwind, and the wind comes out
> to shake the branches which tremble. . . . The earth
> evaporates into dust and flies away. . . .

                                                              (83)

At some distance from the dancers are the nonparticipants who
merely observe from windows which the poet describes as holes (the
reader may again be reminded of the title *La Lucarne ovale*).
Although the movement becomes increasingly violent, threatening to
destroy the entire setting, the dance itself is an opportunity for unity,
for communication. Those who do participate in the ball are no longer
indifferent, but rather attempt to establish a relationship with *others*,
even though their motive is desperation—"Les bras sont des crampons
que l'on jette au premier venu dans le tourbillon du naufrage" ("The
arms are clamps which one throws to the first arrived in the whirlwind
of shipwreck"). This last line of the text, then, aligns the connotation
of the term "whirlwind" with that which it displays in the previous
poems, "Droit mers la mort," where it signified an abrupt, unexpected
death, and in "Les Vides du printemps," where the twisting of the
deserted streets traced the outlines of the nullifying pit, its circular/
spherical shape suggestive of total erasure. The theme of death experienced in the context of a shipwreck and associated with the figure of
the whirlwind or even intense wind, is far more prevalent in later collections of Reverdy's poetry.

Also associated with the violence of a spinning wind is the theme of
dispersal, that is, of the instability and dissolution of the poem's setting.
In another poem from *La Lucarne ovale*, "Le Sang troublé" ("Disordered Emotions"), violent movement has already begun the destruction of whatever surroundings formerly existed. The immediate setting, reminiscent of that in "Les Vides du printemps" but much more
violent, is an abyss, the outlines of which form a circular path shaped
by the twisting, lashing wind. The motion of dispersal becomes more
specific—a window pane is displaced from its frame, a wine bottle

mysteriously appears having no real context whatsoever. Moreover, there seems to be no link between the forceful disengagement of these objects and the poet or wanderer. All are unable to find an appropriate niche in this "paysage sans cadre," a sketch of a countryside with no particular setting.

Affected by the incoherence of the setting, the mind of the poet begins a disordered rambling. Numbers in his head, in imitation of the circular twists of the wind, create their own whirlwind. Further hallucinations reveal a preoccupation with the movement of extension— the path continues endlessly before him, a shadow on the wall stretches itself up to the ceiling. The horizontally extended path and the lengthened vertical shadow intersect, the crossroads indicating more indecision, accentuating the absence of a relationship between the poet and his world.

As noted above, there is an indication of a human presence, but it is rendered impersonally by the pronoun *on*. Perhaps the poet is not fully conscious of what is happening around him, or if he is, he has little interest, given the indifference of the human element which precludes his participation:

> On entend venir quelqu'un qui ne se montre pas
> On entend parler
> On entend rire et on entend pleurer
> Une ombre passe

> You hear someone come who does not show himself
> You hear speaking
> You hear laughing and you hear crying
> A shadow passes

> (85)

The indefinite pronoun "quelqu'un" intensifies the nebulous identity of the pronoun "on." With the repetitious formula defined by "on + verb + infinitive" and the alteration of margin, Reverdy emphasizes the feeling of distance between the person speaking and the action reported. The shadow which represents the only possible tangible source for human interaction quietly slips out of the scene. Human presence is always heard, seen, felt, but never directly experienced. The restrictions imposed upon human relationships by the figures of the elongated wall and path are in the final line of the text re-created by the presence of the shutter, still another barrier: "Les mots qu'on dit derrière le volet sont une menace" ("The words spoken behind the shutter are a threat" [85]). Destroying a final attempt to discover some coherence within the text, such negative communication completes the mood of alienation and results in the complete rupture of setting.

C. *Motion Neutralized*

The destruction of setting does not always occur in the presence of a whirlwind; it sometimes results from a neutralization of initiated movement. It is a remembrance of times past in the text "La Réalité immobile" ("Immobile Reality") which gains the reader entrance into the "neutral state," the scene where mobility is transformed into immobility. Recalling the past, the poet reconstructs a tableau in which many people are journeying toward a house, perhaps his house:

> De tous les champs par tous les chemins
> Les gens arrivent
> . . . .
> Une voiture emplit la route de poussière
> La maison est bientôt pleine d'étrangers
>
> From all fields by all roads
> People arrive
> . . . .
> A car fills the road up with dust
> The house is soon filled with strangers
> (86–87)

Using a series of oppositions as a framework for the poem, Reverdy prepares the reader for the principal contrast of mobility/immobility. The action of the verb *emplir* is neutralized by that which it accumulates, "poussière," "dust," nothingness. Another reversal occurs as the adjective *pleine,* bearing a positive connotation, is opposed by the substantive *étrangers.* Both the street and house, while literally full, are figuratively empty.

Time, too, ceases to exist. Although the clock in the house stops, the visitors awaken; yet no one moves. Dusk, introduced at the beginning of the poem as a moment propitious to memory, will never recur: "Il n'y aura plus de nuit" ("There will be no more night" [87]). The movement of people and objects proceeding forward abruptly ceases, yet paradoxically continues, for the gestures are recorded—"C'est une vieille photographie sans cadre" ("It is an old photograph without a frame/setting"). The absence of a frame in a sense reinforces the absurdity and superficiality of the captured setting, the artificiality of those gathered, yet still in another sense implies that there is no set- ting—every principal movement has been negated or reversed; there can be no reconstruction of the past if the present becomes a fixated neutral state.

D. *Liquid Effacement*

The themes of dissolution and deterioration are not always presented through the setting, but sometimes are treated in association with the figure of the cortege or funeral procession. Unlike previous poems in which this figure has appeared, as in "Cortège" of *Poèmes en prose*, the funeral procession in the text "Jour monotone" ("Monotonous Day") is associated with liquid images especially, connoting an out- pouring, a flowing, a streaming movement toward death. Before the cortege even appears, the liquids water, gas, alcohol, and wax from a burning candle become causes of destruction:

> A cause de l'eau le toit glisse
> A cause de la pluie tout se fond
> Le pétrole l'alcool et ma faible bougie
> Ont incendié la maison
>
> Because of the water the roof slips
> Because of the rain everything dissolves
> Gas alcohol and my weak candle
> Have set the house ablaze
>
> (93)

Near the house there are flowers, more precisely *black* flowers, their color signifying blood and most likely death. Intense suffering like that of Christ on the cross is introduced with the additional presence of thorns and blood-stained hands.

As the funeral procession appears, it is accompanied by "a slow song" ("une lente chanson"), again suggestive of an outpouring of emotion, a flowing of tears. The linear aspect of the cortege is greatly minimized in comparison with the preceding "Cortège," the only allu- sions to line being the procession itself, the road along which it passes, and the house and window of the dead woman. When the procession has passed, there is silence, with one exception, the sound of the rain, falling down, away to death: "On n'entend pleurer que la pluie" ("You only hear the rain crying" [94]). The circular shape of the poem's structure re-creates the same liquidity of motion with which the poem opened.

E. Linear Effacement

The figure of the cortege does not always occur in *La Lucarne ovale* in the context of liquid movement and dissolution. In one final example of this poetic motif from the text "Les Corps ridicules des esprits" ("The Ridiculous Bodies of Minds"), Reverdy reverts to the preoccupation with line and with linear passage previously displayed in *Cale sèche* and *Poèmes en prose*. Throughout this prose poem, more people progressively join the procession, lengthening the line and filling the empty space which stretches on ahead: "Un cortège de gens. . . . Quelques-uns sourient dans le vide. . . . Les plus petits en queue" ("A cortege of people . . . . Some of them smile in the emptiness. . . . The smallest ones at the end" [132]). Emphasis upon the motion of passage is obtained from the repetition of the verb *passer* and references to linear elements of the itinerary:

> On passe. . . . La route s'illumine. . . .
> On passe. . . .
> Bientôt, c'est un boulevard bordé de cafés. . . .
> Le cortège a grossi.

> They pass by. . . . The route lights up. . . .
> They pass by. . . .
> Soon, it is a boulevard bordered with cafes. . . .
> The cortege has grown larger.

As the procession passes the narrator, however, there is one element which in conjunction with this poetic motif has not previously received emphasis—the effacement of the text itself. The cortege continues along its route, gradually disappearing, gradually erased by distance, and with its disappearance that of the text follows. The procession, then, constitutes the text, it *is* the text; the poem likewise becomes the object, and as the one vanishes, so must the other: "Enfin par l'avenue qui monte la file des gens s'éloigne, les derniers paraissent les plus grands. Les premiers ont déjà disparu" ("Finally by the avenue which climbs the file of people draws away, the last ones appear the tallest. The first ones have already disappeared" [132]). The physical death of the individual and the aesthetic demise of the text are, as in the poem "Droit vers la mort," viewed as one. However, in this former poem it is especially the fragility of the text which is emphasized, whereas, in the present text, it is the interchangeability between the poem and the object which the poet chooses to put into relief.

The violent movement which begins in this collection, introduced by the whirlwind, or by intense liquid motion, the entrapment and suffocation, and neutralization presented in the sequestering images of walls, windows, streets; the dissolution and rupture of setting, and even of the poem itself—all these are suggested in the final lines of the text "Ruine achevée" ("Ruin Completed") which serves perhaps an an epilogue to the entire collection: "Un pan de décor qui s'écroule/Dans la nuit" ("A section of decor which collapses/In the night" [107]).

IV   La Liberté des mers (*Freedom of the Seas*)

The formative years of Reverdy's career close with a collection of prose poems, *La Liberté des mers*,[30] many of which were composed during 1915–1916, but not published until 1960. Accompanying this intimate meditation on life and art, are colored lithographs done by Jean de Bazaine, Georges Braque, Marc Chagall, Fernand Léger, Henri Matisse, Joan Miró, Pablo Picasso, and Georges Rouault. The tone and mood of the poems remain the same as those of the later texts of this first early period: deeply philosophical, intensely lugubrious. Even at such an early point in what was to be a long career, Reverdy anticipates death, the ultimate destination of the traveler which begins to haunt him unremittingly. Yet, death will be dominated and ultimately vanquished through art.

At the beginning of one untitled text, Reverdy establishes the tone and mood by repeating the sound [myɤr]—heavy, sad, expressive of a downward motion:

Mur*mur*es entre les quatre *murs*, aux gouttes de sang des épines, comme en allant cueillir des *mûres*, dans les sentiers gonflés de remords et d'espoir aux risques des pentes peu sûres.

Murmurs between the four walls, in drops of blood from thorns, like while going to gather mulberries, in the paths swollen with remorse and hope at the risk of uncertain slopes. No page number; the underlining is mine.

The sound [mɔ̃r] as in "remords" is closely related to that of [my̆r] and likewise emphasizes weight and sadness. Once again as in previous poems, the poet is emprisoned between four walls—whether a room or a building from which there emanates only murmurs, barely audible, distinguishable sounds, nothing precise or completely meaningful. The presence of blood and thorns implies violence and suffering endured by the poet as he struggles to create, and perhaps, restitution for the past mistakes, certainly confirmed in the substantive *remords*. Although there remains an element of hope, it is countered by the presence of uncertain slopes or directions.

Coupled with the anguishing problems of his craft, the artist must confront an ever-present transformation which is a basic component of life, and one which, indeed, may result in self-doubt and an absence of self-understanding. Reverdy finds it futile to try to know his fellowmen or even his environment. Better to travel to the end of the path and resign oneself to the ultimate destination.

Yet the bitterness of the above passage is balanced by the faith the artist puts in his craft, and the ability of art to ultimately counter death:

Comme il y a une étroite bordure ensoleillée aux rivages des mers qui nous fait oublier les immensurables étendues et la profondeur insondable des abîmes—de même, chez les hommes, il y a tout autour de l'immensité obscure qui garde les morts sans écho, les plages dorées de la gloire.
C'est sans doute pour ça que l'on peint et que l'on écrit.

As there is a narrow, sunny border on the banks of the seas which makes us forget the immeasurable expanses and the fathomless depth of the abysses—so, with men, there is all around the obscure boundlessness which guards the dead without echo, beaches gilded with glory.
It is without doubt for that that one paints and writes. No page number.

Juxtaposed to the boundless, the unlimited, and the immeasurable is the precise, artistic detail, with its known dimensions of character, theme, and style. There is, then, a solution to the collapsed settings and uncontrolled violence of the final poems from *La Lucarne ovale:* it is the collection itself, and all those which precede and follow. Like Malraux many years later, Reverdy views art as an "anti-destin," a force worthy of confronting destiny and capable of insuring the survival of certain monuments to human meaningfulness, the triumph of mortal energy over the immortal meaningless void.

CHAPTER 3

The Nord-Sud *Era, 1917–1918*

T HE years 1917–1918 marked a period of exploration for Reverdy. Beginning with the journal *Nord-Sud*, Reverdy published his first work of aesthetics containing experimental theories of imagery, punctuation, and syntax. The new literary trends which Reverdy introduced there not only foreshadowed his later style but also greatly influenced avant-garde French poetry. More aesthetics followed in *Self defence* and other new genres appeared in *Le Voleur de Talan*, considered either a novel in poetic prose or a long prose poem. This last work provided Reverdy with an opportunity to emphasize a new system of typography which he had developed earlier as well as to vent his growing unrest, a symptom perhaps of his later religious crisis. Less original in inspiration was the collection of prose poems, *Au Soleil du plafond* (*In the Sun of the Ceiling*) and parts of *Les Jockeys camouflés*, both works composed under the influence of futurism and cubism. Yet the latter also revealed some of Reverdy's more developed poetic figures, such as the wall and the void, in addition to the theme of effacement. The most well-known collection of the period, *Les Ardoises du toit*, presented this theme with an even stronger negative interpretation. In this same collection, Reverdy further developed the use of linguistic locations and explored the theme of movement with poetic figures of passage such as the threshold. At the close of this period *La Guitare endormie* appeared, continuing an emphasis upon motion which had been started in *Les Ardoises du toit*, movement with and without logical basis or purpose.

I   *First Aesthetics*

A.   Nord-Sud

Representing the modern spirit of the new century, Reverdy sought in the establishment of the literary review *Nord-Sud* (*North-South*) to provide a common ground of understanding not only for his own work but also for that of the other young poets of his day. Conceived in the spring of 1917, *Nord-Sud* was to verbalize and record those aesthetic theories which, Reverdy felt, needed explanation and clarification. Besides Apollinaire, who had urged Reverdy to found the journal, Paul Dermée, a poetic disciple, served as advisor and secretary. Financial aid was derived principally from Jacques Doucet, a wealthy couturier and patron of the arts, and a friend of Max Jacob. Additional support came from a Norwegian named Halvorsen and very possibly from the Chilean poet Vicente Huidobro, and possibly from Apollinaire himself.[1] Generally, the review was composed of articles concerning art and literature, reviews of poetry collections, and anecdotes about some of Reverdy's contemporaries. Only Reverdy's most important articles will be discussed here, namely, those concerning poetic creativity, the relation between poetry and the various art movements of the day, the prose poem, and elements of the "new" poetry.

One of the most important essays of the journal appearing in the first issue is entitled "Sur le cubisme" ("On Cubism"). This essay deals with what constitutes creativity in art, not only in painting but in poetry as well. Cubism, the author finds, is " . . . un art de création et non de reproduction ou d'interprétation" (" . . . an art of creation and not of reproduction or interpretation" [17]). The essence of creation lies in the distinction between *object* and *subject:* the painting itself, or the creative means used to produce it now becomes the subject, and the object(s), once considered the subject, is seen only in its eternal and constant qualities, i.e., the roundness of a glass, etc. The anecdotal aspect of the object(s) is, therefore, abandoned (17–18). Apollinaire as early as 1913 in his *Les Peintres cubistes* (*The Cubist Painters*) interpreted the cubist refusal of the anecdote and the representational subject: "La vraisemblance n'a plus aucune importance, car tout est sacrifié par l'artiste aux vérités, aux nécessités d'une nature supérieure qu'il suppose sans la découvrir"[2] ("Verisimilitude no longer has any importance because everything is sacrificed by the artist to truths, to necessities of a superior nature which he assumes exists without discovering it").

Reverdy places himself in direct opposition to the naturalists' attempt to duplicate objective reality. The reader may recall the poems "Carrés" from *Quelques poèmes*, discussed above. The objects within these poems have little or no relationship with their environment; the few recurring elements relate to sound, not to anecdote: for example, the term *gouffre* repeated in "Je passe en m'engouffrant, je m'engouffre en passant. Quel gouffre!" ("I pass by as I am being devoured, I am swallowed up as I pass. What an abyss!" [66]) or the term *reliure* quoted in "De la reliure de tes lèvres de la reliure de tes volets de la reliure de nos mains" ("From the binding of your lips from the binding of your shutters from the binding of our hands"). The real subject of the poems is their newly created linear shape as arranged by the poet on the page. As a result of excluding experiential context, according to Reverdy, the subject, i.e., the totality of poems, achieves an existence of its own, independent of reproduction or imitation. It is this independence and process of becoming that gives art its reality, artistic reality, Reverdy insists, and not realism which is imitation.[3]

Further development and explanation of Reverdy's ideas regarding cubist theory are set forth in the fourth issue of *Nord-Sud*, that of June, 1917. Looking back to the symbolists, he acknowledges in the "Essai d'esthétique littéraire" ("Essay on Literary Aesthetics") their efforts to achieve an art independent of the confines of everyday existence (41). Writing, for Reverdy, is not necessarily telling or narrating (" . . . qu'écrire n'est pas forcément *raconter*" [42]). In terms of literary substance the recounting of the *real* event has been replaced by the *created* event.[4] The description of a real event renders art subordinate to reality, thereby reducing it to mere sham, or pretentious imitation: the highest quality of imitation results in the most inferior quality of creation.[5] What then is creation? It is not imagination; the artist should not set out from his interpretation of a fact but rather from the idea that he has of the artistic means at his disposal. Once artistic creation has occurred, it should produce a "purely artistic emotion," not a sentimental or melodramatic one (45–46).

Emotion ("Émotion"), in fact, is the title and subject of a later essay in the eighth issue of the review, dated October, 1917. In more specific terms Reverdy points out that it is a commonly held belief in poetry that themes of sadness and melancholy are found to be more artistic, more expressive or imaginative, to the exclusion of those of gaiety and happiness. Yet, art should produce its effects in a completely different way than by means of any of these sentiments (56). Moreover, the highest form of artistic emotion is a sense of mystery emanating from a work for which there is seemingly no explanation as to how it was composed (60). Emotion, instead of being communicated, should be generated.[6] As emotion emanates from a particular work, the reader's reaction is one of surprise. Reverdy in the last issue of *Nord-Sud*, number sixteen, dated October, 1918, states that the value of a work of art is derived from the quantity of surprise produced and the length of the effect.[7]

Throughout this same text Reverdy is again preoccupied with the exclusion of narrative in artistic composition. The serial novels ("romans feuilletons"), he observes, are born of the spoken word; yet, the principal characteristic of literary art is to be conceived and realized in written form (52–54). Upholding the Flaubertian ideal, Reverdy sought to create something from nothing (" ... *de rien faire quelque chose*"); recording, reproducing, and interpreting were no longer valid (56).

Although Reverdy served as spokesman for the cubist painters in "Sur le cubisme," it was his objective to avoid creating an art solely derived from the aesthetics of cubism. In the same essay he advised that literary techniques applied to painting and vice versa could only result in the appearance of novelty, or, in fact, facile imitation (16). Despite frequent traces of cubist influence throughout his early work, at least through the period of *La Guitare endormie* (1919), Reverdy ultimately achieved an art of far greater dimensions than the cubist perimeters set forth in the aesthetics of *Nord-Sud*. Nevertheless, several of the basic tenets of cubism were permanently adapted by Reverdy and were incorporated into his later aesthetics and poetry, although by that time further developed and used in a different context, especially in terms of psychology and verbal effect.[8]

It is, therefore, not surprising that Reverdy refused to accept the title of "cubist poet." Nor was it only cubism that seemed to threaten the artistic independence of Reverdy's poetry. Contemporary poets and critics labeled his work futurist, and again, Reverdy vehemently protested. Reverdy viewed this art movement as a nationalist awakening in Italy, a resurging of artistic energy which had so far produced "little art" (23). The "Chronique mensuelle" ("Monthly Report"), which appeared in the second issue of *Nord-Sud*, dated April 5, 1917, revealed Reverdy's irritation: "On nous a appelés futuristes et néo-futuristes. ... ici nous ne sommes rien moins que futuristes" ("They have called us futurists and neo-futurists. ... here we are nothing less than futurists" [23]). Futurism was actually only a brief moment in Reverdy's poetry, for the most part, influencing only *Les Jockeys camouflés* (1918) and a few other scattered poems such as "Tentative" previously discussed. With the exception of these two sources, the futurist themes of the machine age and those of glorified violence— war, revolt, and conquest, do not appear in the poetry of the *Nord-Sud* era, nor for that matter, thereafter. In addition, Reverdy's refusal

of the anecdote or narrative found no counterpart among the poems
of the futurists.[9]

Unlike Reverdy's independence with regard to cubism and futurism,
was his admission of a great debt to several predecessors who had been
among the first to develop the prose poem. It was in the third issue of
Nord-Sud of May 15, 1917, that Reverdy acknowledged the contributions to this genre of Aloysius Bertrand, Charles Baudelaire, Oscar
Wilde, and especially Arthur Rimbaud.[10] Rimbaud, in particular,
according to Reverdy, had done the most to give the contemporary
prose poem its shape and structure (34). It was not only acknowledg-
ment that Reverdy had in mind in his recognition of the illustrious
precursors of the prose poem, but also a riposte to Max Jacob's asser-
tions that he himself had invented this genre. In addition, Jacob
claimed that Reverdy's prose poems were imitations of his own work.
Reverdy, who had chosen the prose poem as a medium for his *Poèmes
en prose* (1915) and many of the poems in *La Lucarne ovale* (1916),
maintained that he had instead drawn his inspiration from the nineteenth-century prose poem tradition and particularly from the work of
Rimbaud. Moreover, Reverdy believed that he himself had made the
greatest contribution in the development of the prose poem since the
work left by Rimbaud (249). The friction caused by the arguments
relating to the paternity of the prose poem was to ultimately lead to
the deterioration of the friendship between Reverdy and Jacob.

After exploring the various relationships between the "new" poetry
and other art movements, together with the ideals and conflicts among
the poets themselves, Reverdy set out during the second and last year
of *Nord-Sud* to enumerate the principal poetic elements of the poetry
of this era. It is perhaps Reverdy's image theory for which he is most
remembered in these essays, one which most certainly had a great
effect upon French poetry of the 1920s and thereafter. The image theory was originally announced in the opening issue of *Nord-Sud* in an
essay entitled "Son de cloches" ("Sound of Bells") and written by Paul
Dermée who helped to manage the review. It is believed that Reverdy
coauthored the essay, the objective of which seems to have been to
proclaim the death of the symbolist movement.[11] Later, in the thir-
teenth issue of March, 1918, Reverdy himself wrote an essay entitled
"L'Image" ("The Image"), devoted to this theory.

The image was to be a pure creation of the mind, the mind being
an intuitive faculty contributing to the powers of the intellect and to
those of the emotions.[12] It was born not of comparison but of the jux-

taposition of two more or less remote terms. The more distant and just the relationship between the two terms confronted, the stronger the image would be—the more emotive power and poetic reality it would have. Two terms which had no relationship could not be placed together productively. If the two terms were contrary, they would bear no relationship to one another; they would only remain in opposition.[13] Greatness was not derived directly from the image, but rather from the emotion aroused. The strength of the image was, therefore, in proportion to the strength of its emotion. Such a created emotion was considered pure, for it had resulted from a new confrontation of which only the mind had seized the relationships (74–75).

The immediate origin of Reverdy's image theory can be traced to a discussion between Reverdy and André Breton concerning an article by Georges Duhamel. Treating the relationships of ideas, Duhamel comments that " . . . plus une image s'adresse à des objets naturellement distants dans le temps et l'espace, plus elle est surprenante et suggestive" (" . . . the more an image addresses itself to naturally distant objects in time and space, the more surprising and suggestive it is" [282]). Moreover, again in another article of 1913, entitled "La Connaissance poétique" ("Poetic Knowledge"), Duhamel calls attention to the distance between the two terms, "Plus les idées ainsi combinées se seront trouvées primitivement lointaines, plus l'effet de leur réunion sera saisissant" ("The more the ideas thus combined will be found primitively remote, the more striking the effect of their confrontation will be" [282]). It is more than likely that Reverdy adopted Duhamel's ideas and then further developed them.

Yet Duhamel was not the sole source of inspiration. Baudelaire, too, believed the image to be a "creation of the spirit." However, unlike the creation of Baudelaire, that of Reverdy occurs in an absence of context. Instead of an environment of universal harmony, Reverdy's creation has no life outside of itself. It is not the result of intellectual abstraction (that is, comparison), but rather, a constructive and synthetic process in which both the poet and the reader must participate: the poet must locate the proper objects or terms and the reader must perceive the necessary relationships among them.[14] In addition, books on poetic aesthetics of the nineteenth century such as Joseph-Victor Le Clerc's *La Nouvelle rhétorique* (*The New Rhetoric*) advised that metaphors were inferior if the relationship was not natural enough, or if the terms in question aroused ideas which were incongruous.[15]

There were also other more contemporary sources. The idea of distance between the two terms to be confronted had already been advocated by Marinetti in his manifesto of 1912 (281). The same disparity of terms appeared in Apollinaire's *Les Peintres cubistes:* " . . . des sensations artistiques uniquement dues à l'harmonie des lumières impaires" (" . . . artistic sensations uniquely due to the harmony of different/distant lights").[16] Moreover, Reverdy's elimination of context finds its counterpart among the cubists. The terms of Reverdy's images often bear relationships which have no given existential meaning or, if they do, the contexts are constantly changing. If the latter situation prevails, the images overlap with the result that the new context is continuously annulled by that which is about to follow. The perpetual replacement of context brings to mind analytical cubist painting in which several visual contexts are superimposed one upon the other by planes oriented in different directions. There is, essentially, no real context because as one experiential impression begins, it is superseded by another such impression resulting from a randomly intersecting plane.[17] It is for this reason that Reverdy's imagery up until 1919 and especially just before and during the *Nord-Sud* era, is sometimes called "static," again a characteristic of cubist art.

Reverdy's definition of the image can, in fact, be considered a link between cubism and surrealism, for while it is in part derived from the former, it greatly influenced André Breton in his formulation of surrealist doctrine. Acknowledging his debt to Reverdy, Breton quoted Reverdy's image theory in his first surrealist manifesto (*Manifeste du surréalisme*) of 1924 as he discussed the surrealist image. The destruction of context found in Reverdy's poetry appealed to the surrealists, for they were interested in poems independent of existential reality which were, in a sense, "simply given."[18]

Besides imagery, *Nord-Sud* also introduced Reverdy's ideas concerning the punctuation and syntax that the "new" poetry would assume. The essay entitled "Note: Ponctuation" ("Note: Punctuation") in the eighth issue of the *Nord-Sud* of October, 1917, defends the suppression of punctuation, a technique used by Apollinaire in his *Alcools* of 1913. It is an innovation which, Reverdy feels, contributes "une clarté nouvelle" ("a new clarity") to a given work.[19] Apollinaire, on the other hand, had confided in an interview that by abandoning punctuation, he provided more elasticity for the lyrical context of his vocabulary (269). Reverdy in the same text suggests that with the adoption of new typographical arrangements, punctuation may be deleted

(62). In addition, by varying margins and spaces between lines and paragraphs, parts of the poem could be meaningfully divided or joined. Mallarmé and Apollinaire had already adopted this technique. Moreover, the futurists had also suppressed punctuation, but Reverdy contended that *Nord-Sud* had gone much further, replacing punctuation with typographical dispersions.[20]

The new word placement facilitated a more simple syntactical arrangement. Reverdy's "Syntaxe" ("Syntax") of the fourteenth issue from April, 1918, replies to the criticism that the poetry of the *Nord-Sud* era had suppressed syntax.[21] According to Reverdy, syntax should be appropriate to the literary expression in question; there was no one arrangement of language for literary creation. With the advent of the new poetry came a greatly simplified syntax, by no means suppressed; it above all levied itself against complication and excessive refinement (*"complication* et *alambiquage"* [81]). The precise characteristics of the new syntax were disclosed later in *Self defence* but the style of the essay "L'Image" offered a sample of Reverdy's later composition: short paragraphs tightly linked without the support of conjunctions or adverbs.

Reverdy's essays, then, constituted an introduction to the aesthetics of the "new" poetry. Besides Paul Dermée and Max Jacob, other major collaborators of the review were Louis Aragon, André Breton, Philippe Soupault, Vicente Huidobro, and Tristan Tzara. These last four poets were especially influenced by Reverdy—Aragon, Soupault, and Breton subsequently taking the direction of surrealism, and Huidobro that of "creacionismo." It was in fact the question of influence which caused frequent quarrels between Reverdy and Huidobro. This last, a Chilean, was accused by Reverdy of having plagiarized his work while Huidobro insisted that some of the poetry he had composed prior to his arrival in Paris showed striking similarities to the later *Nord-Sud* style. Reverdy with his supporters maintained, on the other hand, that none of the works in question could be found in editions printed before Huidobro's arrival in Paris.[22] At any event, the poetry by Huidobro published in *Nord-Sud* greatly contributed to the development of "creacionismo" in Latin America. Tzara, a Romanian, who in 1916 had established the dada movement in Zurich, contributed his poems to *Nord-Sud*, thereby introducing dada to Paris (123). Although the review was short-lived, it accomplished a unifying effect in a relatively short period of time. By offering to the avant-garde elements of two eras—those of 1914 and of 1919—and the chance to publish their first serious works, it joined two generations heretofore torn by war and literary dissent.

B. Self defence

Self defence[23] completes Reverdy's aesthetics inspired from the years 1917–1918. A collection of aphorisms relating to literary theory and criticism, it further explains the synthetic faculties of the mind, introduced in *Nord-Sud*, together with the abandonment of conventional reality and syntax. Although not published until the end of the year 1919, it is associated in tone and content with the *Nord-Sud* period, stressing the preference for a more simplified, authentic approach to poetic composition rather than the needlessly complicated, artificial interpretations of tradition.

The mind as a source of both intellectual and emotional energy continues to preoccupy Reverdy. Elaborating further, Reverdy explains in *Self defence* that the intelligence becomes aware of certain levels of reality and the emotions, in turn, become aroused by them; the mind assimilates and incorporates them ("L'Intelligence prend connaissance des réalités, la sensibilité s'en émeut; l'esprit les assimile et les admet"). There is no *artistic reality* without the mind ("Il n'y a pas de *réalité artistique* sans esprit" [105]). In order for artistic creation to occur, two aspects of the mind must interact—the first is the dream, and the second, thought. The latter is the more aggressive, or in Reverdy's words, " . . . l'esprit qui pénètre" (" . . . the mind which penetrates"); the former more passive, " . . . l'esprit qui se laisse pénétrer" (" . . . the mind which lets itself be penetrated" [106]). This less aggressive element predominates in the mind of the poet whose receptivity becomes the subject of a deeper analysis in the later work *Le Gant de crin*.

Again inspired by the cubist notion of banishing existential reality from the canvas, Reverdy applied this theory to his vocabulary. Instead of the conventional connotations, words and phrases were to be washed clean, denuded in effect, and brought back to their primitive semantic states. It was from this cleansing that the purity and integrity of the poem would be derived (120). Mallarmé had already employed this technique, and Francis Ponge would adopt it much later after Reverdy.[24] The purging of assigned and arbitrary semantic properties demanded restraint and moderation, and again for Reverdy, as for the cubists, there could be no art without a sense of discipline (121). Reverdy's support of discipline may be interpreted as a criticism of the dadaists who at this time vehemently advocated the complete disintegration of all linguistic conventions, the abolition of logic, memory, and accepted sign systems.[25]

The extensive simplification of vocabulary was paralleled by that of syntax. Whereas in *Nord-Sud* Reverdy had only made brief mention of his views for the "new syntax," in *Self defence* he elaborated upon several ideas concerning syntactical combinations in the construction of imagery: direct confrontation or juxtaposition of the poetic elements instead of using an intermediary term like *comme* or other metaphorical equivalents such as adjectives which only weakened the image and reduced its clarity.[26] Although Reverdy minimized his use of adjectives, he did not suppress them. Such syntactical changes reminded many critics of the futurist programs which advocated the abandonment of all verbal forms but the infinitive, in addition to the deletion of the adjective, adverb, and other connectives, terms of metaphor, or conjunctions. In comparison with the syntax of the futurists, Reverdy's revealed only limited modifications.[27]

II Poetry of Transition: Thematic Divergence

A. Le Voleur de Talan

A little-known work of 1917, *Le Voleur de Talan* (*The Thief of Talan*) incorporated the ideas of poetics and style announced in *Nord-Sud* and *Self defence*. This text was poorly received by the contemporary literary audience, perhaps because of its new typography, that is, constantly varied spacing of text from the margin.[28] Reverdy came upon the idea for this work after a visit with Max Jacob during which he became curious about some papers which Jacob had left in an open trunk. Having observed Reverdy's interest, Jacob abruptly closed the trunk. Jacob, according to Reverdy, often seemed obsessed with the idea that other writers would plagiarize his work. The thief, then, of Reverdy's title is one of talent, appearing in the term *Talan* which phonetically is the same as that of *talent* ("talã" [175]).

Yet the material for *Le Voleur de Talan* draws upon more than just Reverdy's relationship with Max Jacob. It is in effect a description of some of Reverdy's experiences during his first months in Paris. Although the work may be a novel, and is most certainly descriptive and at times enumerative, Reverdy, as he asserted in *Nord-Sud*, has avoided anecdote; instead of telling a story, he has juxtaposed elements of several incidents and has described his emotional reactions to them at later, isolated points.

The beginning of *Le Voleur de Talan* reflects many of Reverdy's previous texts: a traveler arrives in Paris as did the author from his native Narbonne. His first impressions record an atmosphere of reserve and ambiguity—smoke, fog, colorless surroundings.[29] In contrast to the frenzied sound of a train and automobiles are the motionless buildings and silent, uninviting grey sky of the city. Perhaps the one unifying figure in this text is the Seine whose slow, measured current repeatedly links those points along its shores and transports their cargoes. It is not until this part of the text that a friendly presence is introduced as an acquaintance of the beleaguered traveler. For the time being, the loneliness of the isolated wanderer ends, and he greets a person who will later be known as Le Mage Abel or Max Jacob.

Jacob's welcome friendship now explains the terms which the poet uses to describe his new friend: "En naissant/un éclair avait nimbé/sa tête" ("While being born/a flash of lightning had haloed/his head" [11]). Reverdy portrays him here as a Christ figure who had saved him from unhappiness. Yet, it is very possible that this description is not to be taken seriously, that Reverdy's manner may be slightly tongue in cheek, for Jacob widely discussed his dramatic views of having been "saved" and "born again" into Catholicism. Whichever interpretation is accepted, it is clear that Jacob introduced Reverdy to many of the prominent figures of the Parisian artistic community. To avoid the use of anecdote to re-create this experience, Reverdy juxtaposes elements of several conversations occurring sequentially in different locations. With no transition whatsoever, pieces of conversation from a bar where they are sitting are cited alongside phrases exchanged as they later walk up the foggy rue Ravignan in Montmartre. The ascent of this street where Reverdy had once lived reinforces the idea of a newly begun voyage into a more intellectual sphere, indeed, the exact opposite of the "familiar abyss below" spoken of in the preface. The sharp contrast of isolation and sudden friendship, together with an absence of transitional material to frame the conversation in the bar and again on the street bring to mind the technique of collage which Reverdy had so successfully adopted in "Carrés" of *Quelques poèmes* the year before.

As the ascent of the rue Ravignan continues, an emphasis upon line becomes more prevalent; the immediate surroundings are defined solely by line and create a restricting and in fact, imprisoning atmosphere. Without transition, Reverdy passes from the walk up the rue Ravignan to a time three months later when the Mage visits him in his room in Montmartre. Again, just as abruptly the visit is over and Reverdy finds himself alone observing the anonymous movements of *others*. As in the poems of *Quelques poèmes* and *La Lucarne ovale*, [30] there is no interaction with other people; the poet merely looks on— someone ("quelqu'un") passes by his room, shadows appear on the walls across the way, lights can be seen between the doors—yet none of these instances results in a direct encounter.

In a later chapter the young poet returns the visit, only to be cast by the Mage into the role of thief. The use of the term *Mage* suggests Jacob's confidence that he himself could serve as a guide and model for literary creation as well as for a mystical sense of inner peace. As in the incident which Reverdy later related to Maurice Saillet, when he arrived unannounced at the Mage's apartment, he apparently startled Jacob, who then sought to hide all the papers that had been lying on the table. Reverdy was subsequently given the title of "Le Voleur de Talan"—"the Thief of Talan" or "talent."

Jacob's paranoia is even more evident as Reverdy, returning from selectively spaced free verse to poetic prose in paragraph form, humorously discloses the Mage's fear:

> On pourrait se retourner brusquement et voir
> s'envoler quelque oiseau noir en forme d'homme
> avec un manuscrit ou un livre sous le bras
> mais on n'aurait pas pu le retenir
>
> One could brusquely turn around and see
> take flight some black bird in the form of a man
> with a manuscript or a book under his arm
> but one would not have been able to hold him
>
> (37)

The fast rhythm of the fourth line contrasting with the slower pace of the first three lines, where each word is set off with a long space, emphasizes the idea of flight. The Mage would indeed have his literary audience believe that much of the poetry published by *others* had been derived from his genius in one form or another.

Unsure of his craft and misunderstood by his colleagues, the poet's sense of isolation intensifies. In one of two conventional prose passages,

he vents his feelings of despair against the thoughtlessness and cruelty
of the rest of the world, Jacob and anyone else he had quarreled with
included:

> . . . La consolation qui eût pu lui venir de sa grande jeunesse laissait la place
> au désespoir que lui inspirait l'éternité du monde et la cruauté de notre pas-
> sage éphémère. Jeune, il se sentait vieux et savait qu'il ne jouirait pas de la
> renommée qu'il peinait à atteindre.

> . . . The consolation which might have been able to come to him from his
> great youth gave way to despair with which the eternity of the world and the
> cruelty of our short-lived passage inspired him. Young, he felt old and knew
> that he would not enjoy the fame which he was toiling to attain. (65)

This passage foreshadows much of Reverdy's later life—quarrels with
his close friends, Apollinaire, Gris, Jacob, and Cocteau, and still later—
unsuccessful attempts to gain recognition for his poetry. Again in anticipation of his future, the solution, he thought, was to withdraw within
himself, thereby eschewing all confrontation and conflict: *"Il faut
fermer les yeux et se boucher les oreilles car, en nous, tout est vérité,
mais il ne faut vouloir persuader personne"* (*"It is necessary to close
your eyes and ears because, within us, everything is truth, but you
must not want to persuade anyone"* [68]). Several years later Reverdy
would withdraw to a quiet, secluded life at Solesmes, where he could
devote himself to God and his writing craft.

Yet for the moment the poet decides to resume his efforts to com-
pose. It is again the Mage, his learned friend, who becomes the subject
of his thoughts. Having reassumed the role of a Christ figure, the Mage,
thought to be dead, will be resurrected in three months. While his
friend has disappeared from the ordinary, commonplace world, the
young poet is humourously described as having plunged into the half-
opened trunk in order to seize literary secrets. He refers to openings
and unlimited spaces which, of course, occur in association with
another voyage. However, the actual present is too limiting, too restrictive. Explaining that still more space is required, the poet confides that
the voyage is not a memory but instead a dream—

> On se sent attiré parfois par un plus grand espace
> Le besoin de voir plus loin que le mur d'en face

Il faut un paysage plus grand

En fermant les yeux

One sometimes feels drawn by a larger space
The need to see further than the wall opposite

It is necessary to find a larger landscape

By closing one's eyes

(97)

It is a voyage, however, of disunion, for its stages interrupt his thought process: "Des morceaux d'univers s'écartent/Des blocs s'écrasent" ("Pieces of the universe move apart/Segments collapse" [98]). The theme of Reverdy's world being torn asunder now begins to develop; it will become one of the most important aspects of his later poetry, especially in *Ferraille* and *Flaques de verre*. Although believed to be therapeutic, each voyage brings to mind memories of previous failures—"Si je pouvais oublier que j'ai vécu ailleurs" ("If I could forget that I have lived elsewhere" [98])—and for that matter, a few moments of success which will perhaps not recur—"Où étais-tu toi-même/Rien n'indique la trace de tes pas" ("Where were you yourself/Nothing indicates the trace of your steps").

As Reverdy resumes the description of his friendship with Jacob, the voyage abruptly ceases. The Mage has by now awakened, or if the interpretation of the Christ parallel is preferred, he has arisen. Still paranoid, the Mage returns to his search for and careful examination of papers which he believes *others* have stolen. Then, without warning, individual anger is transformed into universal holocaust. Again anticipating the mood of *Ferraille* and *Le Chant des morts*, the theme of global destruction not only refers to the war which had not yet ended, but also to the psychological unrest within Reverdy himself. He chooses verbs denoting falling ("tomber"), flowing ("couler"), cutting ("trancher"), or in the extreme opposite sense, those indicating no motion at all—"cesser." Often there is violent movement with unknown cause: " . . . derrière quelque chose/menaçait de tomber/ sur nos têtes" (" . . . behind something/threatened to fall/upon our heads" [109]). When the forces of rupture cease, nothing will remain

except blood—"Après les coups seront plus forts/Tous les fleuves ces-
seront de couler/Il n'y aura que du sang partout et cc/sera fini"
("After the blows will be stronger/All the rivers will cease flowing/
There will only be blood everywhere and it/will be finished"
[111]).

If the scenes of global destruction do refer to the personal unrest of
the poet, then they may perhaps be given a more positive interpretation, that is, a total purging or cleansing of his mind. As the text nears
its end, a whirlwind begins to form around the Mage who is about to
undertake a new journey. The train station is, however, deserted;
blood-stained doves have just died, tears have been shed. The door of
a monastery opens, beckoning: the Mage is starting on a voyage toward
death (his own death) or perhaps from death—that is, leaving the
death of the world: "Le monde ressusciterait peut-être" ("The world
would revive perhaps" [124]). As he nears the boundaries of the monastery, figures of restriction again impose themselves upon him:
" . . . la limite du cloître et de la/liberté" (" . . . the limit of the cloister
and of/liberty" [125]). Reaching his destination, he has arrived at a
port of grace; the mystery and unpredictability intrigue him as in an
adventure to the other end of the world. The crossing has been completed, but has it ever really happened? And has the Mage ever really
lived? Reverdy now returns from all journeys and all dreams to the
world of the commonplace and ends the text simply: "Le Voleur de
Talan qui avait voulu/vivre vient de mourir" ("The Thief of Talan
who had wanted/to live has just died" [127]). The existence of the thief
is now in doubt; perhaps all along he was just a figment of the Mage's
imagination as indeed Jacob's fears of plagiarism were a figment of his.
And the text and the moments of creativity, had they really occurred
too, and, if so, what had they produced? The text, in effect, foreshadows Reverdy's withdrawal to Solesmes in 1926 and his own personal
admission that "Nous n'avons jamais pu trouver de place au soleil qu'en
nous-même" ("We have never been able to find a place in the sun
except within ourselves" [160]).

In addition to foreshadowing thematic material which would reappear in Reverdy's later, more mature work, *Le Voleur de Talan* exem-
plified several of the newer means of artistic expression discussed at
length in *Nord-Sud* and in *Self defence*. With the exception of Reverdy's previous prose poems of *Poèmes en prose* and several in *La
Lucarne ovale*, he had already abandoned all punctuation in his
poetry. *Le Voleur de Talan* continues that approach, excluding two

long prose passages conventionally punctuated. Yet, what was newly illustrated in this last text was Reverdy's liberty with the margin which provided its own punctuation, and the new, simplified syntax expounded upon in *Self defence*. In all his earlier poetry he had respected the ever-uniform right-hand margin with few exceptions. However, with *Le Voleur de Talan* and then *Les Ardoises du toit* and even later, the elements of the poem are significantly arranged on the page among clusters of blank spaces. On page fourteen of *Le Voleur de Talan* the distances from the margin and spaces between word groupings indicate thought sequence and priority:

> La Seine coule calme et lente entre les ponts
> se répétant à l'infini
>
> > Le long du quai on n'avait plus
> > qu'à suivre le courant
> >
> > > Les bateaux qui dessinaient
> > > des vagues sur le fleuve
> > > en lui rappelant la mer
> > > l'émerveillèrent

> The Seine flows calm and slow between the bridges
> repeating to infinity
>
> > Along the quai one had
> > only to follow the current
> >
> > > The boats which drew
> > > waves upon the river
> > > recalling to him the sea
> > > amazed him

The repetition of the calm movement of the river is the dominant thought; supporting it are the locations of the quai and the boats from which points the current and the waves emphasize onward flow. Merely restating the description of the first supportive phrase, the second is placed under it, showing its inferiority. Another example of Reverdy's spatial arrangement occurs as two lateral thoughts, each of equal importance but in a different world, evolve simultaneously:

Un homme chante

Sa barbe est comme un

nuage où brillent encore

quelques gouttes d'eau

La pluie

La lumière éteinte   On cherchait à ses

Le bruit   pieds la couronne
Tout ce qui vibre   d'épines
        dans ma tête

En regardant   Au bas de la cour la porte
                                  où l'on frappe en vain

A man sings

His beard is like a

cloud where there still shine

several drops of water

The rain

The light extinguished   One searched at his

The noise   feet for the crown

All that which vibrates of thorns
        in my head

While looking   At the bottom of the courtyard the door
                                  where one knocks in vain

                                                          (81)

Another example of word arrangement will be repeated in the poetry
of *Les Ardoises du toit* and even further on:

Et puis
> plus rien
>> La nuit

And then
> nothing more
>> Night
>> (85)

The descending arrangement of three-syllable clusters—"Et puis," "plus rien," "La nuit"—accentuates the action of slippage and provides a natural punctuation. Finally, when all has disappeared, there is only the calm darkness of night [nyi], expressed more strongly with the repetition of the sound [yi] in "puis" [pyi].

The extremely restricted syntax advocated in *Self defence* is illustrated in *Le Voleur de Talan* by an elimination of unnecessary adjectives and other modifiers as well as conjunctions. One favorite formula is the grouping of the impersonal third-person pronoun *on* followed by a modal plus infinitive. After the sequence has been repeated several times (especially in *Les Ardoises du toit* and later on), the poet terminates the thought abruptly, usually with an expression that suggests something contrary, or at least unexpected:

On voudrait courir

On voudrait partir
> Ailleurs

One would like to run

One would like to depart
> Elsewhere
> (62)

The second line is a repetition of the first except for the sounds [part]; because of this general uniformity, the great distance suggested in the term *Ailleurs* is somewhat unexpected. Similar in composition is the arrangement

Il y en a qui crient
Il y en a qui prient
> avant de mourir

There are some who cry out
There are some who pray
before dying
(90)

the phoneme *p* being the only difference in the first two lines, until the
third, equally powerful as the *Ailleurs* above because of its position of
isolation. The action of dying is closer in thought to that of crying out
and praying, whereas, the *Ailleurs* provides more contrast, suggesting
distance itself. Like the preceding formula, the sequence "Il y en a qui
..." will recur throughout *Les Ardoises du toit*.

B.   Au Soleil du plafond

Written concurrently with Reverdy's first aesthetics is a collection of
poetry, derived both directly from cubist and futurist influence, and
more originally, from the poet's own personal torments, the thematic
content from which would ultimately become the principal source of
his better known work. *Au Soleil du plafond (In the Sun of the Ceiling)*[31] contains twenty prose poems, punctuated, and in paragraph
form. The poems, most of which were probably written by 1917,
accompany and describe eleven lithographs by Juan Gris. Although the
text itself was composed earlier, this work was not published until 1955.

Intended in hommage to Gris, this work is based upon a series of
lyrical descriptions re-creating Gris' tableaux. The titles alone immediately disclose the cubist preoccupation with everyday objects and
scenes: "Moulin à café" ("Coffee Mill"), "La Pipe" ("The Pipe"),
"Papier à musique et chanson" ("Music Sheet and Song"), "Homme
assis" ("Man Seated"). The reader will also observe that there is a general absence of motion; as with many of Reverdy's cubist poems,
immobility is preferred to mobility. Yet, despite the largely cubist
inspiration, the poems of this work do not generally refer to the geometric arrangement of objects or to the superimposition of planes, both
of which are so characteristic of *Poèmes en prose* and *La Lucarne
ovale*. The more intellectual character of these two former collections
is replaced here with an emphasis upon harmony, a harmony intended
to complement and accentuate Gris' art, but not to rival it.

Though less original in inspiration, *Au Soleil du plafond* does contain references to several figures which the reader will by now recognize as typically Reverdian. Perhaps the most recurrent is that of the

wall, already suggested in the title of the collection, the ceiling being interpreted as a limit beyond which access is forbidden. Perhaps intended as the source and center of the poet's creative efforts, the sun is the focal point of his restricted existence; although a positive force, it can also be viewed in a negative sense as the light which discloses the presence of a barrier. As for the poems themselves, the wall is again frequently seen as a restricting surface or as one upon which scenes are projected. Examples of the former interpretation are found in the poems "Musicien" ("Musician"), and "Homme assis." In the first poem the wall appears as a curtain whose existence is emphasized by its actual spatial dimensions. Later, in the same poem the linguistic location *entre* is associated with the term *mur*. The poet, positioned *between* the hollowed-out walls ("les murs en creux" [54]) is unable to truly perceive signs already presented (53–55). Barriers suddenly appear in the second poem, "Homme assis," and progressively create the background: "Les murs sortent des lignes et coupent l'horizon." ("The walls come out from lines and cut the horizon" [78]). Closely associated with past memories, the wall in the text "Masque" ("Mask") serves as a screen upon which scenes from the past are replayed and reflected in a mirror: "Et même dans la glace contre le paravent. Ma mémoire en désordre" ("And even in the mirror against the screen. My memory in disorder" [139]). Rarely, however, are barriers crossed and unimpeded motion permitted. Yet, one such example is found in the poem "Violon" ("Violin") in which feet keep time to music as obstacles and barriers are passed by.

In addition to the role of objects, barriers also occur in *Au Soleil du plafond* as linguistic locations which are frequently associated with the context of hostile anonymity. As he glances out from the wall, the poet is intimidated by the unknown, aloof faces which are unwilling to interrupt their movement onward. Locations described as "au delà de" ("beyond"), "derrière" ("behind"), or "à côté de" ("beside") are inaccessible to the poet and are inhabited by anonymous objects and people. Against a static background detailed only by heads, shoulders, and eyes, the poem "Eventail" ("Fan") introduces movement initiated by Reverdy's unidentified and equally inaccessible "quelqu'un" ("someone") in an adjoining room: "dans la pièce à côté" ("in the room beside" [90]). Then a face is mentioned, "un visage fermé" ("a closed face"), one which shows no interest in a relationship.

Hostile attitudes on the part of *others* do not always occur in the context of closed doors, shutters, houses. Sometimes hostility and willful separation appear in association with a seemingly true aperture which ultimately is found to be false. The figure of the lamp in the poem "La Lampe" ("The Lamp") of *Au Soleil du plafond* functions as a counterweight to the force of the wind, a source of separation and destruction: "Le vent noir qui tordait les rideaux ne pouvait soulever le papier ni éteindre la lampe." ("The black wind which was twisting the curtains was not able to raise the paper or extinguish the lamp" [93–94]). The verb "tordait" refers to the twisting, violent turning of the wind, so reminiscent of the recurring "tourbillon" ("whirlwind"). In this particular poem, the aperture is an unwelcome one, for it is forced and not undertaken with the resident's wishes: "Dans un courant de peur, il semblait que quelqu'un pût entrer. Entre la porte ouverte et le volet qui bat—personne!" ("In a current of fear, it seemed that someone could enter. Between the open door and the shutter which bangs—no one!" [94–95]). However, the opportunity for interaction has been refused; no one has come in. Although the presence of the wind has been adversely experienced, that is, the table has been shaken, the lamp stands firm as a reliable counterforce—"Et pourtant sur la table ébranlée une clarté remue dans cette chambre vide." ("And yet on the shaken table a brightness stirs in this empty room" [95–96]). The effect of the whirlwind is violence and isolation; what was once filled with life is now a void.

The void is also a figure which will haunt the poet until it reaches its summit in *Ferraille*. Sometimes seen as a hole or abyss, the void often represents death. The lamp, on the other hand, probably refers to the poet's faith in his own creativity which can transform the instability of reality into an ostensibly controlled experience. His mobility severely restricted, and rarely interacting with other people, the poet lives in a vacuum; his prevailing mood is one of insecurity: " . . . dans l'incertitude où nous sommes de vivre si près du ciel sans pouvoir le toucher." (" . . . in the uncertainty where we are to live so close to the sky without being able to touch it" [7].) Every desired object or activity seemed to be just out of the poet's reach, at least at this particular time; he is withdrawn and restricted to the confines of his psychological self.[31]

C.   Les Jockeys camouflés

Although containing several references to futurist influence, *Les Jockeys camouflés (Disguised Jockeys)*[32] is a richer work of much more originality than *Au Soleil du plafond*. Reverdy has incorporated into the text many of his own images and poetic figures, later considered the basic source of his poetry, together with futurist allusions to speed. Throughout the work, an alternation of dream and everyday reality predominates. The text consists of three principal poems, "Les Jockeys mécaniques" ("Mechanical Jockeys"), "Autres jockeys, alcooliques" ("Other Alcoholic Jockeys"), and "Piéton" ("Pedestrian"), all unpunctuated with the exception of an introduction to the second poem which is in punctuated poetic prose. When published in 1918, the text itself was illustrated by Henri Matisse.

The first poem, "Les Jockeys mécaniques," describes a race through the present and perhaps into the future between someone referred to as "lui" ("he") and many "cavaliers" ("horsemen"). Another human presence is mentioned, that of "quelqu'un" ("someone") who appears once and remains unknown. The race is presented as a long voyage by boat, train, and horse, the purpose for which is never revealed. The solitary traveler proceeds by boat, while the horsemen ride; those who will take the train are never identified. As the race begins, the setting of the poem changes from the boat to the train and finally to the horses. Speed is not glorified for the purpose of rushing into the newly mechanized age as in futurist texts, but rather as a means of escaping the present. A momentum is built up as the race-voyage-pursuit unfolds across the sky. When the horsemen as a group unexpectedly descend, their movement becomes disordered. It is no longer a mere descent but rather a true fall: "La dernière chute éclaboussa le mur où se/ posaient les taches claires de la nuit" ("The last fall spattered the wall where/clear stains of night were set" [11]. The use of the verb *éclabousser* intensifies the speed of the fall. Once again, as in *Au Soleil du plafond*, the wall functions as a screen. The terms "les taches claires de la nuit" are an example of Reverdy's imagery; clear, transparent stains seem incongruous with night, yet the compatibility of these terms is explained in the following line, "Tout le reste était dans l'ombre" ("All the rest was in shadow"). Framed or outlined by shadows, the stains represent the remains of the riders, identified in the next few lines as jockeys. It is very possible that the jockeys themselves never existed, but are shadows or reflections of shadows of the oncoming night.

The intense speed in the first text has almost completely disappeared in the second entitled "Autres jockeys, alcooliques" ("Other Alcoholic Jockeys"). Although the race continues, it is a minor element compared to the importance accorded the person, possibly the solitary boat passenger whom the poet addresses as "tu." This second text blends to an even greater degree elements of the dream with those of everyday reality. As the poem begins, motion is kept to a minimum. The theme of eternal passage along a route is modified here somewhat as random groups of people and their possessions progressively form a cavalcade, slowly increasing in speed and density. With no transition, the throng of travelers is left behind, and one solitary voyager becomes the center of attention. The momentum built up by the procession ends, for this one traveler now finds himself in front of a wall, a boundless wall.

As the voyager pushes onward with the wall still in front of him, he may try to enter a structure, a railroad station as in this poem. Yet, each time he attempts to enter, he is unsuccessful: "La porte s'ouvre sur le vide" ("The door opens into a void" [15]). Interpreted as a wall or partition, the door is a successor to the wall; it opens, in contradistinction to the wall, yet again there is only a false opening. The void it leads to is as conducive to immobility as the wall. Two lines later, the door is replaced by the curtain, a form of portal for the human conscience:

> Le rideau et la conscience tremblent
> Qu'y a-t-il derrière
> La crainte nous laisse immobiles
>
> The curtain and conscience tremble
> What is there behind
> Fear leaves us immobile
>
> (15)

Is it fear of what lies in the psychological sanctuary that immobilizes the poet, or fear that nothing lies behind the curtain, hence a continuation of the void? The reader can only wonder. Abruptly the poet reenters the world of everyday reality. Walking along, his thoughts are lost amid half-extinguished street lamps. Perhaps it was this very scene which the poet transformed into falling jockeys and splashing stains, the entire spectacle played out on the wall.

Further references to barriers continue. As the next section begins, the falling rain leads the poet off again into his imaginary world. Seen as bristling, the rainspouts seem almost animalistic. As the water flows more or less uncontrolled, the rainspouts appear to be fleeing fences or restrictive partitions, again replacements for the wall. Used in conjunction with the term *palissade* is the linguistic location *derrière*; it is *behind* such partitions that plots ("complots") are woven ("se tramer"). The function of the preposition *derrière* here brings to mind linguistic locations in *Au Soleil du plafond*—a place near but not accessible to the poet, of which he knows but can never see. The choice of the terms "se tramer" and "complots" foreshadows Reverdy's extreme paranoia of his later years.

As the poet begins to reenter the world of everyday reality, he wonders what exactly has changed. All appears the same but the poet realizes he has been somewhere and witnessed change—the path upward no longer leads to the washhouse, the once departing boats return and put away their sails as they pass under the bridge. The poetic text has reached its end, as has the voyage: "Ne regarde pas nous sommes au bout de la ligne/et il faut descendre" ("Don't look we are at the end of the line/and it is necessary to descend" [18]). Replacing the wall, the term *la ligne* identifies the boundaries of the creative world which must be crossed and left behind. As the descent progresses, the temperature drops; whatever memories the poet has brought back with him from his dream will now remain suspended or frozen in time: Il fait froid/Le feu se refroidit dans les glaces où/il reste pris ("It is cold/The fire grows colder in the glasses where/it remains prisoner" [18]).

The theme of race and pursuit has given way in the third and last poem of the collection *Les Jockeys camouflés* to that of a long, slow journey described in terms of lines and based upon the motion of passing and turning. All references to the fast approaching horsemen have been abandoned. The title of the poem "Piéton" ("Pedestrian") introduces the only identifiable character in the poem, perhaps the same person as the solitary boat passenger and the evening stroller in the previous two poems. As the traveler moves along the road, his attempts to interact with *others* are thwarted:

> Il y a des bras dans la rue qui s'étreignent
> Des mains dans le jardin
> Des plaies qui saignent
> Il y a des murmures dans le vent
> D'où viennent les voyageurs qui passaient
> sur le chemin

> There are arms in the street which grasp each other
> Hands in the garden
> Wounds which bleed
> There are murmurs in the wind
> From whence come the travelers who passed
> along the way
>
>   (20)

Night comes and the poet sleeps. Entry into dream is interpreted as a return home—"Je rentre" ("I go back home"); as each memory recurs, its lines cross those of other previous events, creating a linear network into the past:

> Les chemins se croisent aussi vite en même temps
> . . . .
> Entre deux dates rapprochées tout s'efface
>   1920–1900
>   Si tard
>
> Roads cross as fast at the same time
> . . . .
> Between two juxtaposed dates everything is erased
>   1920–1900
>   So late
>
>   (24)

Reaching and grasping temporal sanctuaries is now preferred to the glorification of speed. Terminating in a more positive sense than either of the first two texts, "Piéton" refers to the effacement of the text and poet into a fertile past where creativity was possible. Effacement in the other two texts had either occurred as death ("Les Jockeys mécaniques") or as the creation of a tormenting void ("Autres jockeys, alcooliques"). Later, in *Ferraille* and in *Le Chant des morts*, the theme of effacement will predominate, not a positive one as in "Piéton," but rather a negative one of destruction and violent movement.

D.   Les Ardoises du toit

Reverdy's work during the *Nord-Sud* era displays much variety in thematic derivation. From allusions to his early experiences in Paris (*Le Voleur de Talan*) to the influence of past or present literary move-

ments (*Au Soleil du plafond, Les Jockeys camouflés*), Reverdy evolves
to a more personal style of poetry, more original, more self-derived.
The collection *Les Ardoises du toit* (*Slates of the Roof*),[33] written in
free verse and published in 1918, represents the pinnacle of Reverdy's
early poetry. Composed of eighty-one unpunctuated poems, with varied spacing and margination, it was a written confirmation of the
poetic style Reverdy had prescribed earlier in *Nord-Sud* and would
later expound upon in *Self defence*. Moreover, what he had borrowed
previously from the futurists and cubists had by this time become his;
it was a work of which he put more of himself than ever before.

A consistent figure in Reverdy's poetry, the wall has been associated
with temporal change in several previously discussed poems. Throughout *Les Ardoises du toit* the association is broadened, including not
only the terms "shutter", "curtain," or "fence," but also that of "eyelid" (*paupière*). In the poem "Cadran" ("Sun Dial"), no doubt remind-
ing the reader of the text "Piéton" ("le cadran l'arbre et l'aiguille"),[34]
the eyelid serves as a curtain which delineates diurnal and nocturnal
time:

> La moitié se ferme
> 　　　Et le ciel
> 　　　　　　Se couvre
> 　Un lourd rideau qu'on ouvre
> Sans bruit

> One half closes
> 　　　And the sky
> 　　　　　　Becomes overcast
> 　A heavy curtain which one opens
> Without noise

> 　　　　　　　(172)

The shorter lines, that is, the second, third, and fifth suggest the action
of blinking. Contrast, initially provided by the verbs "se fermer/se cou-
vrir" and "ouvrir," is repeated in the lines that follow:

> 　　　　　Une lumière luit
> 　Rapide
> 　C'est une autre lueur à présent
> 　　　qui me guide

> A light shines
> Rapidly
> It is another glimmer at present
> which guides me

Confirming the aperture of day are the substantives "lumière" and
"lueur." In another poem "L'Ombre du mur" ("The Shadow of the
Wall") the arrival of night is interpreted as withdrawal or retraction:
"Le monde rentre dans un sac/la nuit" ("The world returns to a bag/
At night" [198]). Temporal indication in the poem "Matinée" ("Morn-
ing") is indicated by the size of a shadow—

> Une étoffe irréelle
> C'est peut-être une autre dentelle
> A la fenêtre
> Qui bat comme une paupière
> A cause du vent
> L'air
> Le soleil
> L'été
> Les traits de la saison sont à peine effacés

> An unreallike material
> It is perhaps another piece of lace
> At the window
> Which blinks like an eyelid
> Because of the wind
> Air
> Sun
> Summer
> The traits of the season are scarcely erased
> (220)

Although unmentioned, the pane itself becomes a screen upon which
temporal divisions are indicated, whether they are parts of the day or
portions of the year. The choice of three short nouns—"L'air/Le
soleil/L'été" together with their spatial arrangement suggests again as
in the text "Cadran" the action of blinking. Reverdy's new typography,
as in Le Voleur de Talan, is an integral part of the poetic structure.[35]
The eyelid then serves as an instrument for registering temporal
change, indicating the hours that have ticked by, and then erasing
them, starting anew.

Further development in the theme of temporal passage in association with the wall is found in *Les Ardoises du toit* as Reverdy centers his attention upon the threshold between the two states in question, day/night; present/past; dream/everyday reality. Whereas in "Piéton" and other previous texts, the passage of night into day is expressed as an event, in *Les Ardoises du toit* Reverdy emphasizes the location or setting of the events, the state of transition instead of accomplished action. Abundant indications of the exact nature and setting of transition, lacking in most previous texts, are found in substantives such as *seuil* ("threshold"), *paupière* ("eyelid"), *rideau* ("curtain"), *barrière* ("barrier"), *porte* ("door"), and *rive* ("bank"). The threshold in the poem "Route" is one linking the present to the past; yet passage across this line of demarcation cannot even be attempted owing to the presence of a barrier:[36]

> Sur le seuil. . .
> . . . .
> Qu'y a-t-il derrière
> > Un mur
>
> > > des voix
> . . . .
> Au moment où je passais là
> Et tout le long une barrière
> > Où sont ceux qui n'entreront pas

> On the threshold. . .
> . . . .
> What is there behind
> > A wall
>
> > > voices
> . . . .
> At the moment when I was there passing by
> And all along a barrier
> > Where there are those who will not enter
> > > (176)

Contrary to other previous texts of *Au Soleil du plafond* or *Les Jockeys camouflés*, accessibility of memory is nonexistent; memory in the above text is an empty road bordered by a wall along which stand those who are also being denied reentry into their pasts. Movement across the threshold into the past or into dream is again denied in the poem "Une éclaircie" ("A Clearing"): "Je voulais franchir la barrière/ Quelque chose me retenait" ("I wanted to cross the barrier/Something held me back" [180]). Connecting dream with everyday reality, the

threshold in the poem "Le Même numéro" ("The Same Number")
appears as a riverbank (rive), this time a partition providing support or
protection for the privileged world of the subconscious: "Les yeux à
peine ouverts/La main sur l'autre rive" ("Eyes scarcely open/The
hand on the other bank" [205]). Several lines later a door frame forms
a new threshold: "La porte s'inclinait/Une tête dépasse/Dans le cadre"
("The door slanted/A head projects/In the frame" [205]).

Having the same general effect as the figure of the wall, several
recurring locations, most of which are prepositions, reconfirm the
themes of restriction and isolation. The linguistic locations au-delà de,
à côté de, and derrière, although occasionally referred to in Au Soleil
du plafond and in Les Jockeys camouflés, permeate the text of Les
Ardoises du toit. It is the position derrière in the poem "Route" which
conceals the poet's past, pieces of his life he seeks to re-create. In
another text "Cortège" ("Procession") the position behind separates
him from all other human activity—"C'est derrière le mur le plus
épais que tout se passe" ("It is behind the thickest wall that everything
happens" [231]). Again in the poem "Dans les champs ou sur la colline"
("In the Fields or On the Hill") the poet's location is expressed by a
linguistic location, this time by the adverb ailleurs—"C'est à tout ce
qui se passait ailleurs que l'on pensait" ("It is about all that which was
happening elsewhere that one was thinking" [216]). Many poems contain double references to linguistic locations such as the text "Miracle"
in which derrière occurs with à côté. Like the open door in Les Jockeys camouflés, there is an opening which may be entered, yet the poet
too will refuse the opportunity: "La porte se serait ouverte/Et je
n'oserais pas entrer" ("The door would have opened/And I would not
dare enter" [189]). Never explaining his motive, he will forego learning
about the contents of the room—"Tout ce qui se passe derrière" ("All
that which happens behind"). It is behind where others are discussing
the poet; he can hear voices, but understands nothing: "On parle/Et je
peux écouter/Mon sort était en jeu dans la pièce à côté" ("They speak/
And I can listen/My fate was at stake in the room beside" [189]). Further defining derrière, the location à côté ("beside") may remind the
reader of a line from the text "Eventail" of Au Soleil du plafond, "Il
y a quelqu'un qui tourne dans la pièce à côté" ("There is someone who
is turning in the room beside" [90–91]).

The capacity of the location entre to contain and protect is challenged by the force of time in the text "Couvre-feu" ("Curfew").
Underneath a solitary lamp, the poet is attempting to re-create a mem-

ory; it is a setting similar to that of the text "Enveloppe" ("Envelope") from *Au Soleil du plafond*. Yet in this poem, memories are not flashed upon the wall, but rather unfamiliar faces and scenes which seem to blur together. The location of *entre* is, however, one of potential warmth and shelter—"Un coin au bout du monde où l'on est à l'abri" ("A corner at the end of the world where one is sheltered" [224]). Although this potential exists, it is never realized; the memory is fragile, and when exposed to time, crumbles and is erased. No trace is left of the position *entre:*

> Ma figure plus effacée
> Entre nous deux l'air chaud qui tremble
>   Un souvenir détérioré
> Entre les quatre murs qui craquent
>   Personne ne parle
> Le feu s'éteint sous la fumée

> My face more erased
> Between us two warm air which trembles
>   A damaged memory
> Between four walls which crack
>   No one speaks
> The fire is extinguished under the smoke
>   (224)

The use of the first person, "ma," quite common in *Les Ardoises du toit*, suggests a more personal experience and gives the location *entre* an aspect of intimacy. If the poet did recognize anyone from the recreated scenes, those traces together with the text of the poem have yielded to temporal forces of destruction. Contrary to the theme of effacement in *Les Jockeys mécaniques*, here the speed of the movement is not emphasized, but instead its constant, destructive nature. Effacement also occurs in "Autres jockeys, alcooliques" without reference to destruction; the dream and text just disappear. It is especially in *Les Ardoises du toit* that Reverdy begins to emphasize destructive motion, an aspect of his later poetry with which he seemed to be obsessed.

Another linguistic location, introduced much earlier in *Poèmes en prose* ("Les Poètes") but which becomes more predominant in *Les Ardoises du toit* is the preposition *autour de*. The oval or round shape of the lampshade itself in the text "Abat-jour" ("Lampshade") suggests

this location as does the shape of the table. Reference to the lamp was
made in *Au Soleil du plafond* ("Enveloppe"), but not in association
with linguistic locations. The atmosphere created by the location
autour de in this former text is one of warmth and calm, flexibility and
contentment: "Il fait froid dehors/Mais là c'est le calme/Et la lumière
les unit" ("It is cold outside/But there there is calm/And the light
unifies them" [173]). It is in such a setting that the poet will later
attempt to re-create a memory. Past events have already been realized
in the poem "Tard dans la nuit . . ." ("Late in the Night . . ."). Again
the re-creation is associated with the lamp shining upon the table, the
shape of its shade and that of the table inscribing those who take part
in the memory, protecting them, preserving them:

> La table où ils se sont assis
> Le verre en cheminèe
> > La lampe est un coeur qui se vide
> C'est une autre année
> > Une nouvelle ride

> The table where they sat
> The lamp on the mantle
> > The lamp is a heart which empties itself
> It is another year
> > A new wrinkle

> (174)

However positive the memory may seem, it does contain moments of
sorrow:

> Ils sont assis
> > > La table est ronde
> Et ma mémoire aussi
> Je me souviens de tout le monde
> Même de ceux qui sont partis

> They are seated
> > > The table is round
> And my memory too
> I remember everyone
> Even those who have left

> (174)

The adjective *ronde* again emphasizes the unity of the lamp and that of memory. Although re-creation of the past moment is completed, the oval or circular line forming the position *autour de* inscribes the places of those who are absent, either lost or dead. It is in this particular interpretation that the line of the shade and table form a partial void; in this sense the poet/voyager returns from his trip only to find himself again at the point of departure.

Re-creation of the past is often associated in *Les Ardoises du toit* with reflection, carried out upon a mirror or pane of glass. Contrary to some poems in which the theme of reflection permits no penetration, Reverdy in "Rives" ("Banks") associates some movement inward with the mirror. The mirror initially serves as a screen and, like the wall, provides a surface upon which the past is relived. However, it is not just one immobile scene from the past, but instead a series of shots, creating a cinematographic effect:

> Le miroir s'enfonçait
> On y voyait une ombre
> De tous ceux qui sont morts on ne sait plus le nombre

> The mirror was penetrated
> One saw a shadow there
> Of all those who have died one does not know the number
> (194)

From the shadow, one small portion of the past, then to the numerous dead, the poet proceeds eventually to the remembrance of a child crying, the wind rustling, the leaves falling. Memories throughout Reverdy's poetry usually contain some reference to the dead; they are rarely happy moments. As each memory evokes the next, the reader has the impression of entering, and descending into a narrow corridor, being formed at that very moment by the verb *s'enfoncer*. Yet, the great depth suggested by this verb is promptly negated when the voyage downward abruptly ends. Aperture has been limited; as the voyage into the past is completed, the poet has found no one with whom to interact—those who have been alive, the crying child, for example, are obviously unresponsive. The poem ends with the image of a labyrinth, a network of confusion, perhaps possible encounters but yet complicated by unknown events.

Disappointment is again linked with reflection in the poem "Carrefour" ("Crossroads"), with the principal difference that here there is a religious interpretation. From *Les Ardoises du toit* onward, the theme of the crossroads assumes much more importance. A development of the theme of the voyage, it usually connotes an obstacle to be met and dealt with, either in a religious sense or in a purely psychological sense, sometimes in a creative sense. In the temporal setting for the poem "Carrefour," given as "Après la chute ou le réveil" ("After the fall or the awakening" [208]), the term *chute* may refer to either the setting sun or the Fall from Grace, while the substantive *réveil* may indicate the approach of morning, or the Resurrection. Having stopped at the crossroads, a traveler/artist ponders a decision—should he abandon the protection of literary tradition ("Quitter la cuirasse du temps" / "Leave the armor of time" [208]) and seek perfection in a more original style—"Et boire au cristal transparent"/"And drink of transparent crystal")? A ray of sunlight reflected in his glass appears to be a form of guidance, but unfortunately it disappears soon after. The decision to be made may be religious as well as literary; the lines of the crossroads suggest those of the Crucifixion. Yet, no answer is forthcoming; the poet is condemned indefinitely to be a solitary figure:

> Enfin tout seul j'aurai vécu
> Jusqu'au dernier matin
>
> Sans qu'un mot m'indiquât quel fut le bon chemin
>
> Finally I will have lived all alone
> Until the last morning
>
> Without a word having been indicated as to what was the right way

There are several religious poems in *Les Ardoises du toit,* all of which foreshadow Reverdy's spiritual crisis of the 1920s. One such representative text in which religious uncertainty is combined with the poet's fear of the hole or abyss is the poem "Pointe" ("Point"). At the beginning of the text, two directions are given in which the reader may proceed—"Vers le vide ou vers l'ennemi" ("Towards the void or towards the enemy"[190])—seemingly two equally negative options. Human presence suggested by the substantive *l'ennemi* is again anonymous; perhaps the poet has associated it with the rupture of night, disclosed in the ensuing line—"En tombant la nuit s'est fendue"

("While falling night has split"). Rupture connoted by the verb *se fendre* prepares the reader for the tragic Crucifixion scene immediately following and the abyss created at the end of the poem:

> Deux bras sont restés étendus
> Dans l'ombre un regard fixe
>
> . . . .
> Pour aller plus loin vers la croix
>
> Two arms have remained stretched out
> In the shadow an intent gaze
>
> . . . .
> To go farther toward the cross

No certainty exists as to whether within the poet's own mind the crucified Christ may be resurrected, or whether the lifeless stare can be transformed into warm, encouraging guidance. However, the poet's movement toward the cross indicates his willingness to try to believe. The repeated indefinite pronoun + verb structure—"Tout ce qu'on voit/Tout ce qu'on croit" ("Everything which one sees/Everything which one believes")—accentuates his confused state—conflicting religious beliefs which the poet cannot organize. It is a sequence often repeated in *Les Ardoises du toit*. As the poem terminates, the poet's desire to resolve his religious doubts is further complicated by his fear of the void, initially referred to at the beginning of the poem: "Avec la peur d'aller trop près/Du ravin noir où tout s'efface" ("With the fear of going too near/To the black ravine where everything is effaced" [190]). The adverb *trop près* may perhaps be a location for true religious understanding; however, fear of the abyss or nothingness—that is, the nonexistence of a guiding force—may keep the poet from attempting further discovery.

With the exception of certain passages from *Les Jockeys camouflés*, Reverdy's poetry until the collection *Les Ardoises du toit* contains little movement and in many instances—for example, in *Poèmes en prose*, *Quelques poèmes*, and *Au Soleil du plafond*—can be described as static. From *Les Ardoises du toit* onward, Reverdy's preoccupation with motion increases to the point where in *Flaques de verre, Ferraille*, and *Le Chant des morts* his entire universe is ravaged by constant rupture. Sometimes found in close association with an emphasis upon movement is the theme of the abyss which undergoes development in *Les Ardoises du toit*. In addition, Reverdy often interprets the wind and storms as sources of destructive motion. Yet the emphasis is not always upon movement in a negative context, for in some poems he returns to his favorite pastime: observing the constant passage of anonymous travelers.

With the exception of the time of his conversion to Catholicism, Reverdy found religion a disquieting source of doubt. His reservations were seen earlier in his poetry as profound skepticism, such as in the previously discussed texts of "Pointe" and "Carrefour," while later on skepticism hardened into incorrigible bitterness and cynicism. Some of the poems of *Les Ardoises du toit* contain a vein of religious uncertainty deeper than that which would question the existence of guidance. The texts "Entre deux mondes" ("Between Two Worlds") and "Projets" ("Plans") pose the possibility that because of the complete hostility of man's environment, there may be no higher force with any measure of control, or if such a force does exist, it would seem absolutely uncaring. The former text depicts man as a victim of world-wide upheaval, in an abstract sense. The rapid, senseless movement of the earth seems to offer only unpredictable reversal and overthrow—"Personne d'assez grand pour arrêter la terre/Et ce mouvement qui nous lasse" ("No one great enough to stop the earth/And this movement which wearies us" [225]). Again it is the reconstruction of memory, reflected upon the wall in disorder and rupture, then effaced, and then created anew which further isolates the poet, dispersing his identity: "L'ombre danse/Il n'y a plus rien/Que le vent qui s'élance" ("The shadow dances/There is no longer anything/Except the wind which springs forward" [225]). What the poet hoped was a portion of memory is only a shadow blown by the wind; if indeed there was something reconstituted at one time, now there is nothing. The positive connotation of the verb *danser* is abruptly counterbalanced by the negative "ne . . . plus rien que" ("no longer anything except"). As rapid motion reappears with the verb *s'élancer*, the poet treats the movement itself as an object which takes up space—"s'étendre," "se gonfler." It does not matter how long each reflection remains, whether momentarily or longer, for each is meaningless. Constantly proceeding onward, the solitary traveler/poet spends his life waiting for one meaningful moment which would have made his entire search worthwhile.

Further along in the same collection, in the poem "Projets," the relentless movement of the earth, seemingly without purpose, is reminiscent of the line "Le monde fatigué s'affaisse dans un trou" [219]), from the poem "Sentier." A negative context for movement is introduced in the former poem with the verb *ébranler* ("to shake")—sound waves from bell towers shake a once tranquil setting. Again a criticism of a seemingly uncaring God, this text registers its doubt in more specific terms than those of "Entre deux mondes." Human anguish in this particular text is caused by the forced dispersal and subsequent destruction of previously made plans, attempts to give lives structure:

> Et sur le trottoir mouillé glissent
>   Tous leurs désirs éparpillés
> Qui restent morts dans la coulisse
> De l'ombre épaisse où ils sont nés
>
> And along the wet sidewalk slip away
>   All their desires scattered
> Which remain dead in the wings
> Of the thick shadow where they were born
> (232)

It is a natural element, the storm, foreshadowed by the earlier shaking motion, which has transformed attempted order into disorder. The verb *glisser* connotes the quick, smooth flight of ideas; the past participle *éparpillés* emphasizes the force of the wind. Later, during some of Reverdy's moments of deepest depression, the use of the terms *glisser* and *éparpiller* will increase to the point where the settings and objects of most poems escape the poet's/traveler's grasp, leaving him suspended with no context whatsoever to which he can relate. Never having been developed, these thoughts or plans remain lifeless; the terms *coulisse* and *l'ombre épaisse* make reference to Reverdy's frequent use of the substantive *plis*, a location in which new ideas are hatched and incubated. The dilemma of the poet's creative ideas being destroyed before they have even been given the chance to live is again reminiscent of Mallarmé's haunting vision of stillborn poems.

E. La Guitare endormie

One last work associated with this period, *La Guitare endormie* (*The Guitar Asleep*),[37] is in comparison less rich in variety of thematic material, yet in regard to several themes, contains a higher level of literary development. Published in 1919, with artwork by Juan Gris, *La Guitare endormie* actually appears after the close of the *Nord-Sud* era. However, in terms of the poet's attitude and composition, it is closer to this period than to the one steeped in religious crisis and psychological torment which follows. It comprises several poems treating the problems of literary creativity as well as a few other themes in which movement assumes an even greater role. In general, the theme of movement in this collection diminishes in importance, yet of those poems which are structured around mobility, the degree of motion is intense and fast-moving.

Presented as an eternal journey to mark time until some meaning can be discovered in the earth's senseless, uncontrolled movement, as in the text "Entre deux mondes," human existence in *La Guitare endormie* is described as a waiting period, that is, a time of expectation in a creative context, both negative and positive. The theme of *attente/waiting*, having received little attention since "Bande de souvenirs" and "Sujets" of *Cale sèche*, is expanded in this collection. The introductory lines of the poem "En attendant" ("While Waiting") depict the literary dilemma of a poet dissatisfied with an all-too-familiar routine of composition and poetic formulas:

> Des lignes trop usées par les rigueurs du temps
> La flaque d'eau sous la gouttière
> Le reflet timide qui danse
>   Et la nuit qui descend
> Aucun essor
> Aucun effort
> Pour détacher l'esprit de cette ritournelle

> Lines too worn by the severities of time
> A puddle of water under the rain pipe
> The timid reflection which dances
>   And night which descends
> No flight
> No effort
> To detach the mind from this same tune
>   (37)

The puddle of water *is* the timid reflection which merely echoes what has been tried or said before. The descent of night suggests the possibility of access into the realm of *sommeil* ("sleep") or "fantasy." Flight, as the threshold is crossed, whether in the Mallarméan sense, into the azure or in the Reverdian sense, along the interminable route, seems to be the only solution. But for a renewed vocabulary with an emphasis upon the theme of reflection, descent, threshold, flight, the reader would believe himself to be confronting the text "Sujets" from *Cale sèche*.[38]

Despite the poet's repeated efforts to try again, inspiration, if it does come, slips away from the artist. As with Mallarmé, Reverdy uses the substantive *aile* to refer to the fragility and gentleness of the creative moment: "Au passage émouvant d'une aile/Tout s'évapore et sèche" ("At the touching passage of a wing/Everything evaporates and dries" [37]). It is this thoroughly negative attitude which distinguishes the waiting in this text from that of "Sujets," for in the latter text the poet held out some degree of hope for channeling his creative impulses into fruition.

In sharp contrast to this distinctly negative attitude to the theme of *attente*, are two other selections from *La Guitare endormie*. The period of expectation in the text "Filet d'astres" ("Net of Stars") occurs during a voyage by boat, a time during which creative transformation is realized much as it is in the very early text from *Cale sèche*, "Bande de souvenirs." A much shorter poem in comparison, with fewer themes and therefore, much less confusing in the interweaving of thematic material, the text, written in the first person, describes the creative moment in terms of movement—a pure, untouched wave is cut by the rudder of the boat, the sterile surface of a blank mirror is inscribed with a name. As if in a dream, the poet begins to fantasize concerning the journey:

> Un navire indécis navigue vers mes yeux
> Les rayons du soleil tombent en lourdes tresses
>
> . . . .
> Le côté blanc de notre espoir
> Dans l'émouvant et doux sillage de la barque
>
> . . . .
> Quand le chemin s'ouvre et s'anime
> Aux reflets dansants du falot
>
> A blurred ship sails toward my eyes
> The rays of the sun fall in heavy plaits
>
> . . . .
> The blank side of our hope
> In the touching and soft wake of the boat
>
> . . . .
> When the road opens and becomes full of life
> In the dancing reflections of the lantern

(47)

The boat, moving toward the poet, is tossed about in the swells of the waves, vehicles of transition. The terms "tombent en lourdes tresses" again remind the reader of the work of Baudelaire, where in countless poems waves of hair are rapidly transformed into those of water. In the next stanza, the process of artistic transformation focuses upon the virginal creativity of the poet—the pure, untouched side of hope is ready to receive inspiration, unadulterated by preconceptions. The wake produced as the boat plies through the waves, the "émouvant et doux sillage," again brings to mind the earlier poem "Bande de souvenirs" from *Cale sèche* in which foam is introduced as the product of transition in the creative process. Finally, at a propitious moment, aperture does occur, on a lighted boulevard or around the fire from the ship's lantern. The movement of the reflections—their size and shape—now defines the moments of creativity:

> ... plein d'échos
> d'éclairs de lanterne et d'étoiles
> de formes dans la vapeur d'eau

> ... full of echoes
> of flashes from the lantern and of stars
> of forms in the water vapor

(48)

Contrary to the often destructive effect of the wind is Reverdy's interpretation of this force in the poem "Quelque part" ("Somewhere"). Here, in the only text of this collection written in punctuated poetic prose, the whirlwind occurs in the very uncommon context of little motion followed by immobility and linked with the theme of religion and the figure of the crossroads. Actually protective, the wind shelters the clearing in which the travelers have taken refuge—"Le vent en tourbillons aigris garnit le fond de la clairière" ("The wind in embittered swirls protects the back of the clearing" [43]). As the travelers look about, the interaction of the setting sun upon the vegetation appears as a vision of the Crucifixion; the berries and thorns are Christ's blood, the redness of the descending crown His agony: "Les mûres saignent au bord du ciel où grimpent les épines. La couronne du monde enserre le front torturé du couchant" ("The mulberries bleed at the edge of the sky where thorns climb. The crown of the world encircles the tortured forehead of the setting sun"). Movement, suggested by the verbs *saigner, grimper,* and *enserrer* now diminishes and finally ceases. The lines of the sheltered clearing are actually quite delineated; apparent aperture has again become closure—"La haie vive qu'on ne peut pas franchir flambe et brûle les yeux ..." ("The lively hedgerow which cannot be crossed blazes and burns the eyes ..."). As in so many other poems, the hedgerow is an uncrossable threshold which like the wall restricts mobility. However, the action of *flamber* and *brûler* does not have to refer to a destructive context, but rather to a purifying process with salvation in view. This possible interpretation seems even more likely with the introduction of the crossroads—an intersection of roads and the perpendicular arrangement of wood pieces to form the Cross: "Mais au croisement des quatre routes, des quatre membres— ... après l'angoisse du passage le plus serré, le plus étroit, l'arrêt du calme et du repos dans la blancheur de l'étendue et le silence" ("But at the meeting of the four roads, of the four limbs— ... after the anguish of the closest passage, the narrowest, the stop of calm and rest in the whiteness of extent and silence" [44]). Once having moved from the point of intersection, the poet has left behind whatever religious doubts he may once have had; inner peace, indicated in the terms "calme," "repos," "blancheur," "étendue," and "silence" seems to permeate his spirit, at least for the time being.

By the end of the *Nord-Sud* era, Reverdy had developed most of his his principal themes and poetic figures. He would, of course, further rework them, selecting different contexts and combinations, but the distinctive features of his poetry had been set forth: surrounded by either hostility or indifference, the voyager relentlessly pushes onward, traveling by boat, by train, or on foot amid anonymous multitudes,[39] yet always alone. Surrounded by unstable settings which are threatened by rupture and collapse, he seeks to flee into the past or into dream, often thwarted by the paralysis of artistic sterility and death, the restricting lines, or the agent of dispersal, the whirlwind. In terms of aesthetics, Reverdy acknowledged in his prose his gratitude to the past, yet also developed his own theories of poetic imagery, as well as spatial arrangement of text and syntax, all of which are incorporated into his subsequent work. From this point onward, the theme of descent is perhaps the most significant in Reverdy's work. It is ironic, for the poet's ever-haunting fear of the journey downward into the abyss of psychological and religious crisis now becomes the source of some of his most poignant poetry. What he feared most perhaps was the fragmentation of his spirit, in itself paradoxically becoming a source of unity for all who seek to defeat human finitude.

CHAPTER 4

Creation Through Conflict: Religious Skepticism and Subsequent Disillusionment, 1921–1928

ALTHOUGH Reverdy's work during the years 1921–1928 seems surprisingly untouched by his conversion to Catholicism in 1921, the prose and poetry of this period do testify to the skepticism which preceded and the disillusionment which followed his espousal of the new faith. The unstable settings of the earlier *Les Ardoises du toit* continue, victims of sudden change and frequently, of complete effacement. The poet's thoughts are often rambling, especially in the prose of the period where he incoherently records figures of successive nightmares. Throughout both the prose and poetry, God is often depicted as neglectful and indifferent, the one exception being *Le Gant de crin* (*Glove of Horsehair*). An analysis of intense religious feelings, this last work represents a moment of complete inner peace, which, although short-lived, resolved all conflict for the poet. It was a brief respite from the subsequent years of disillusionment and hopelessness.

I Poetry: The Beleaguered Muse

The years 1921–1928 saw little that was new in Reverdy's poetic work. At the beginning of this period, especially through the year 1922, Reverdy composed several minor collections of poetry, less rich in imagination, with little dynamism in imagery. Of the three works, *Etoiles peintes* (*Painted Stars*),[1] *Coeur de chêne* (*Heart of Oak*),[2] and *Cravates de chanvre* (*Ties of Hemp*),[3] the first is a return to the punctuated poetic prose of the earlier *Poèmes en prose*, while the others

96

are unpunctuated, with some varied spatial arrangement of text. Composed and published at about the same time, the two former works appeared in 1921 and the latter in 1922. While the theme of movement is continued and treated in a negative context, earlier figures used by Reverdy such as the lamp, wall, threshold, in addition to linguistic locations appear with lesser frequency. In terms of stylistic differences, the reader will note much less emphasis upon the first person, a repetition of initial terms, and graphic linear arrangement.

A.   Etoiles peintes, Coeur de chêne, *and* Cravates de chanvre

The theme of movement is primarily associated in these three works with an unstable setting. It is particularly in *Etoiles peintes* that Reverdy seems to be preoccupied with the motion of slipping, that is, the unsteadiness of objects and people or the actual effacement of setting and text. Ambiguity of context is suggested by the verb *glisser* ("to slip") in the first line of the poem "Le Monde plate-forme" ("The World Platform"): "La moitié de tout ce qu'on pouvait voir glissait" ("Half of all that which one could see was slipping" [69]). A more specific location is designated in the terms "Le pavé glissant" ("the slipping pavement"). Those in the setting, described as "passants" ("passers-by") have climbed into another world. The verb *escalader* ("to climb"), suggesting the scaled barrier or wall, indicates that the instability of setting may continue.

The ambiguous setting of "Le Monde plate-forme" is completely effaced in the text "Les Mouvements à l'horizon" ("Movements on the Horizon"). Movement continues, again described by the verb *glisser*, but in this particular poem, it is carried out through the medium of water. The scene of horsemen riding along a road, reminiscent of *Les Jockeys camouflés*, is ambiguously described as "C'est une véritable armée en marche ou bien un rêve" ("It is a veritable army in motion or else a dream" [73]). The actions of those who witness the scene are equally uncertain—"L'enfant pleure ou dort. Il regarde ou rêve" ("The child is crying or sleeping. He is looking or dreaming"). When the horses slip into the water, effacement begins: "Les chevaux glissent le long de l'eau. Et le cortège glisse aussi dans cette eau qui efface toutes ces couleurs, toutes ces larmes" ("The horses slip along the water. And the procession also slips into this water which erases all these colors, all these tears"). It is possible that the procession is proceeding

toward death, the ultimate linear journey as in "Au saut du rêve" of
Cale sèche, yet without the mood of doleful resignation of this earlier
text. It would not be a painful, tragic death, but one which cleanses
and purifies, removing inauthenticities and cares of life. This liquid
passage of purification is in direct contrast to the violent, streaming
movement of the verb *glisser* in the earlier poem "Jour monotone" of
La Lucarne ovale. Instead of movement being completely stopped
here, it is perhaps only temporarily neutralized: the procession may
leave the stream. There is not only complete effacement of setting but
also that of text. The cortege *becomes* the poem; when that disappears,
so does the text itself. The interchangeability between the poem and
object(s) brings to mind a similiar treatment in the earlier "Les Corps
ridicules des esprits" of *La Lucarne ovale,* with the principal difference being the preference of the verb *passer* in the latter as opposed
to the verb *glisser* in the former.

In contrast to the gradual, controlled movement of "Les Mouvements à l'horizon," effacement implies uncontrollable violence in the
poem "Mécanique verbale et don de soi" ("Verbal Technique and Gift
of Self"). Here a calm, controlled setting is completely destroyed by
the swift, forceful passage of a train:

Un train passa derrière la barrière et brouilla les lignes qui tenaient le paysage
debout. Et tout disparut alors, se mêla dans le bruit ininterrompu de la pluie,
du sang perdu, du tonnerre ou des paroles machinales, du plus important de
tous ces personnages.

A train passed in back of the barrier and jumbled the lines which kept the
countryside standing. And everything disappeared then, lost itself in the
uninterrupted noise of rain, of lost blood, of thunder or of mechanical words,
of the most important of all these characters. (72)

Disorder, introduced with the verbs *brouiller* and *se mêler,* suddenly
gives way to a deadly liquid outpouring—rain, blood, thunder, words.
Nothing remains of characters or setting. The destruction realized in
this poem recalls that of the texts "Jour monotone" and "Le Sang troublé," both of *La Lucarne ovale,* in which a twisting, lashing wind is
the vehicle of displacement.

In spite of the effacement of the above texts, motion does not dominate the poetry of *Etoiles peintes.* The crossroads, suggesting indecision and immobility, forms the focal point of the poem, "Au carrefour
des routes" ("At the Intersection of Roads"). Once again used in a

religious context as in "Carrefour" of *Les Ardoises du toit*, the intersection of the horizontal and vertical lines forms a cross, toward which a Christ-like figure gazes with hands outstretched and head hung low. As in the earlier "Carrefour," a call for direction or guidance is met with silence. Contrasting with the stationary cross is a burst of sound as an attempt is made to answer Christ: "Une voix d'en haut sortait de derrière un nuage, mais le tonnerre, en roulant, l'a brisée" ("A voice from above came out from behind a cloud, but thunder, while rumbling, broke it" [85]). The identity of the voice is ambiguous, although the term "d'en haut" ("from above") would seem to suggest God. The immobility of the poem is rapidly changed into one movement silenced swiftly by another. The three commas after the terms "nuage," "tonnerre," and "roulant" also add to the feeling of fragmented motion.

As soon as it begins, Christ's plea ends, stifled. The poem closes as it began, with complete indecision and immobility. It seems somewhat contradictory that Reverdy, about to convert to Catholicism, would continue to express serious doubts about God's interest in humanity or about His power to effect change. Such feelings are a continuation of the religious skepticism found in the poems "Pointe," "Entre deux mondes," and "Projets," all of *Les Ardoises du toit*. His attitude is, however, consistent with his loss of faith in formal religion after his arrival at Solesmes.

Strangely, other aspects of the poet's craft occupied his thoughts more at the time of his conversion to Catholicism than the theme of religion. In a text from *Coeur de chêne*, Reverdy explores the technique of enumeration (through structural repetition) as well as that of multiplication. Describing the wind in the text "Le Reflet dans la glace fête foraine" ("The Reflection in the Mirror Traveling Fair"), the poet repeats the third person singular *il* ("it") with a verb of motion, and then varies the locations associated with each verb:

> Il vient des rues fermées du faubourg noir qui
> rampe
> Il vient des boulevards que traverse de loin
> un passant attardé
> Il sort du trou grillé où l'odeur de la ville
> s'engouffre tout le jour
> Il naît et meurt entre les mille murs
> Mais il monte aussi haut et aussi bien que l'air du large

> It comes from closed streets of the dark outlying
> districts which crawl
> It comes from boulevards which a belated passerby
> crosses from afar
>
> It comes out of a grated hole where the smell of the
> city sweeps in all day long
> It is born and dies among the thousand walls
> But it rises as high and also as well as the air of the
> sea
>
> (103)

The succession of nouns which discloses the directions of the wind seems an endless multitude: closed streets, boulevards, sewers, walls. As the passage ends, Reverdy repeats the structure adjective + preposition + noun:

> Plein de lampes
>   de suie
>   et de brouillard
>
> Full of lights
>   of soot
>   and of fog
>
> (103)

Further along in the same poem the reality of life at the fair is analyzed, once again with the repetition of initial terms:

> Ce qui avance ce sont ces têtes innombrables
> Ce qui bouge ce sont ces épaules qui plient sous le
> brouillard
> Et ce qui brille ce sont les yeux vivants des spec-
> tateurs
>
> Those which advance are countless heads
> Those which move are shoulders which bend under the
> fog
> And those which shine are the lively eyes of the
> spectators
>
> (104)

By alternating the repeated expressions "ce qui ... ce sont" with the new terms, Reverdy emphasizes those elements which are occurring for the first time. The successions "avance/bouge/brille" and "têtes/ épaules/yeux" continue the effect of multiplication seen earlier in this poem.

Although the theme of movement does not dominate *Cravates de chanvre*, the last work of the earlier years of Reverdy's religious crisis, it does appear there in a more intense and rapid form than in either *Etoiles peintes* or *Coeur de chêne*. The figure of the whirlwind, so common in the poems of the earlier *La Lucarne ovale* with rare occurrences in *Au soleil du plafond* and *La Guitare endormie*, is once again the source of sudden change and confusion in "Echo" ("Echo"). The force of the wind has altered the customary appearance of a descending curtain, usually connoting a gradual motion downward as night or sleep commences, here unfurling and spreading out of control: "Sur tous ces gestes le vent déroule la nuit/C'est un rideau mobile qui descend" ("On all these gestures the wind unfurls night/It is a mobile curtain which descends" [121]). Whatever was visible before now becomes questionable as having been actual reality; the effects of the whirlwind have begun to be felt: "la route en tourbillon/tous les mirages/la poussière" ("the road in a whirlwind/all the mirages/ dust"). There is confusion among all elements of the setting: " ... les spectacles confondus au jeu les voix mêlées les cheveux embrouillés ..." (" ... spectacles confused in a game mixed voices tangled hair ..."). Verbal communication is incoherent: " ... les mêmes mots sur un autre papier" (" ... the same words on another paper").

Interior disorder parallels the effects of the exterior, destructive wind force, recalling the poem "Le Sang troublé" of *La Lucarne ovale*. In that earlier text incoherent, rambling thoughts disabled the poet's creativity. Here, in the poem "Echo," wanders an echo, disassociated from the rest of the setting while seeking to find the creator of its sound. It discloses its identity and thereupon disappears: "C'est ma voix dégagée/mon nom une lumière les yeux fermés" ("It is my voice separated/my name a light closed eyes" [122]). The last three terms, punctuated by spatial pauses, graphically re-create the echo. It is the poet's own voice, poignantly identified by the rarely occurring possessive adjective *ma*, gradually fading into oblivion or death. With the poet's demise, that of the text follows, just as in the earlier text "Droit vers la mort" of *La Lucarne ovale*, where the downward unfolding of the curtain is again reminiscent of entrapment or burial.

The negative attitude with which Reverdy described the themes of displacement in "Echo" is sharpened in the last poem of the collection, "La Langue sèche" ("Dry Language"). In contrast to the two previous texts, there is little movement in this poem. The poet is trapped in a period of *attente;* his creative *élan* is no longer boundless; its previous flowing motion is now neutralized:

> Tout le chemin est nu
> les pavés les trottoirs la distance le parapet sont
> > blancs
> > Pas de goutte de pluie
> > Pas une feuille d'arbre
> > Ni l'ombre d'un habit
> > > J'attends

> All the road is bare
> the pavement the sidewalks the distance the parapet
> > are white
> > Not a drop of rain
> > Not a leaf of a tree
> > Nor the shadow of a piece of clothing
> > > I am waiting

> > > > (143)

Nudity and sterility characterize the barren mind of the artist, the adjective *blanc* recalling the infertility of Mallarmé's blank page. The rain drop, leaf, and piece of clothing would, if they existed, provide some distinguishable features during the moments of creativity or among the lines of poetry produced.

Despite the paralysis of this waiting period, there is some movement, some lone element of inspiration—"Pourtant le fleuve coule des quais en remontant" ("However the river flows from the piers while rising"). Yet, perhaps because of the poet's mental disorder and confusion, he cannot properly coordinate his thoughts. The poet's attitude toward the period of waiting is as negative here as in the previous poem "En attendant" of *La Guitare endormie:* "la terre se dessèche/ tout est nu tout est blanc" ("the earth is withering/everything is bare everything is blank" [143]). The movement of the river has now been stilled; the implied artistic paralysis as in "Les Poètes" of *Poèmes en prose* suggests that the period of waiting will become nothing more than a void. The poet here recalls the traveler of "Les Vides du prin-

temps;" after repeated attempts to progress, both voyagers are impris-
oned at the initial point of the journey—the beginning is also the end.
One of Reverdy's darkest moments to date, the period of waiting in
"La Langue sèche" does not offer the escape to dream or sleep as in
the earlier *Les Jockeys camouflés*, "Autres jockeys, alcooliques;" in this
particular text there is no other alternative than to attempt to endure.

B. Epaves du ciel, Ecumes de la mer, Grande nature, *and* La Balle
    au bond

Throughout the later years of Reverdy's religious upheaval, he
became increasingly bitter and more resigned to disappointment. Two
years after the publication of *Cravates de chanvre*, an anthology
appeared consisting of all of Reverdy's previously published poetry
from *Poèmes en prose* to this last work. Its title, *Epaves du ciel (Derelicts of Heaven)*,[4] emphasizes the uncertainty and skepticism of its
author. The following year, 1925, another anthology, *Ecumes de la
mer (Foam of the Sea)*,[5] included selections from the earlier *Les
Ardoises du toit*, *La Lucarne ovale*, and *La Guitare endormie*. There
is no extreme change in the thematic material of the later part of this
period as compared with that of the earlier years. The themes of instability, total effacement, religious indecision, divine indifference, and
artistic sterility continue; yet, there is a more pronounced emphasis
upon a fear of the void and of death. Containing several texts in which
Reverdy has maintained the conventional left-hand margin, the collection *Grande nature (Sovereign Nature)*, written with an absence of
punctuation in 1925, is the last work of this period in which a contradiction is apparent between Reverdy's espoused religious feelings and
his poetry. The religious ardor which moved Reverdy to convert to
Catholicism in 1921 and withdraw to the cloistered religious society at
Solesmes in 1926 had already abated by the time *La Balle au bond
(Ball on the Bounce)* appeared in 1928. Reverdy returns in this collection to the medium of punctuated poetic prose. Like *Grande nature*
there is a noticeable decrease in the number of poems which develop
the theme of movement. The occasional religious skepticism described
by Reverdy in *Coeur de chêne*, *Etoiles peintes*, and *Cravates de
chanvre* occurs with much more frequency in *Grande nature* and *La
Balle au bond* in anticipation of the intense metaphysical torment and
deep depression which Reverdy suffered after 1928.

As indicated in the title of the collection *Grande nature*,[6] Reverdy is extensively preoccupied with recurring events in the world of nature: the dawn of day, the approach of night, the passage of time recorded through natural cycles. However, the grandeur and supremacy of nature dwarfs and surpasses human efforts to contribute a lasting monument, or even to survive at best. The mechanized manner in which the natural world operates and its complete indifference with regard to human beings are described in texts such as "Souffle d'ouest" ("Breeze From the West") and "Fausse joie" ("False Joy"). In the former poem the measured onset of night calmly unravels in complete contradiction to the chaos of the human world where people rush driven by fear and tension (11). A few pages later the poet juxtaposes the comfort of the natural world—a city in the south of France warmed by the sun and cooled by the foam of the waves—with the misery of human existence: a carnival in mourning, stifled laughter, silenced steps, the home of the deceased (20–21). The poem "L'Eau Dort" ("Water Sleeps") describes the passage of an entire day with brief mention at the conclusion of a human death (22–23).

Reverdy's general dissatisfaction with his natural surroundings occasionally gives way to deepening depression as in the text "Détresse du sort" ("Anguish of Fate"). Written in a mood of intense skepticism ("J'interroge . . ./J'interroge . . ."; "I interrogate . . ./I interrogate . . ." [17]), the setting of the poem has been molded and shaped by a hand, probably that of God—"Une main enveloppe la terre entre ses doigts" ("A hand envelops the land between its fingers"). However, whatever the identity of this superior force, it seems to have immediately lost interest in its creation—roads which have already been declared impassible are now crowded with throngs and the winter rains, raging out of control, have caused floods and shipwrecks. The narrator of the poem takes comfort in being far from the sea, a source in this text of certain destruction. Unlike Reverdy's early poetry as in "Bande de souvenirs" of *Cale sèche*, the sea no longer offers a potential for creative transformation. It now connotes an abyss where displacement and death are to be expected: "Une suite de collines entoure le creux où l'on voit/se perdre les signaux des lampes d'équipage" ("A series of hills surrounds the hollow where one sees/the signal lights of the ship's gear lose themselves" [17]) A beam flashed from the lighthouse has been the only direction given to those lost at sea and now that, too, gradually disappears: "L'Arc qui entoure ce paysage sinistre et désolé/ perd sa couleur/Je crois qu'il s'use" ("The arch which surrounds this countryside sinister and devastated/loses its color/I believe it is fading away" [18]). If the poet should lose his orienting beam and never escape the abyss, all will not have been in vain, for some portion of his art will remain behind:

Ce qui me rassure un peu c'est que je pourrais tou-
    jours me retenir aux bords
Garder la rampe
Et laisser sur la terre un léger souvenir
Un geste de regret

That which reassures me a little is that I could
    always cling to the edges
Keep to the railing
And leave upon the earth a light memory
A gesture of regret

The intellectual accomplishment, seen superficially as a "light memory," actually constitutes an expression of regret and bitterness before divine indifference. The poet's reliance upon art as a more lasting monument to his own artistic creativity will gradually increase, until, at the end of his life it remains his only hope, unsullied by former disappointments.

There are other moments in *Grande nature* when Reverdy retains no hope whatsoever of leaving behind meaningful traces of human existence. One such text is "N'Essayez pas" ("Don't Try") in which the only clement present is the expanse of the natural world which lies uninhabited save for a memory of those who have fled and the bodies of the dead. The splendor and brilliance of the intense warmth of the sun—"la pédale d'or" ("the pedal of gold"), "La brassée de soleil/ Enflamme le trésor" ("The armful of sun/Sets ablaze the treasure" [24])—is countered by a funereal chill left by those departed—"des villes désertées" ("deserted villages"), "La route est vide jusqu'au ciel/ Le caractère en deuil" ("The road is empty to the sky/The character in mourning"). The degree to which the natural world is unaware of human existence, not to speak of human misery, brings to mind Rimbaud's poem "Le Dormeur du val" ("The Sleeper of the Valley"). Near a singing river, warmed by the sun, a young soldier lies as if smiling in his sleep. The presence of two red holes in his body warns the reader that he is actually dead. Although the natural world is ignorant of his demise, there is at least some interaction between it and the soldier—

his body lies in a bed softened by grass, watercress, and gladiolus.[7] For Reverdy, nature does not react to human death but seemingly isolates itself in a separate sphere of existence.

The poet's preoccupation with the supremacy of the natural world diminishes greatly in the last collection of this period, *La Balle au bond*.[8] His depression deepens as his psychological disorders intensify. Now, events in the natural world, too, occur in a context of fragmentation. As day begins in the poem "La Réalité impalpable" ("Intangible Reality"), fragments of daylight and human features are rapidly swallowed up by the surrounding structures:

On emportait le jour par morceaux dans toutes les rues de la ville. Et les cheveux du vent, mêlés au flot de gens et de voitures, s'engouffraient entre les murs et se nouaient. Tout le monde courait sans savoir vers où.

They carried day along in pieces into all the streets of the city. And hair in the wind, mixed with the wave of people and cars, was swept among the walls and became knotted. Everyone was running without knowing toward where. (71)

Even the comfort which the dream has represented soon subsides as it becomes a bizarre nightmare. The setting of the poem "Le Sommeil du coeur" ("The Sleep of the Heart") recalls that of the early "L'Esprit Sort" of *Poèmes en prose*. In place of the restricting library walls of the latter poem ("De mes ongles j'ai griffé la paroi . . ." [43]), is a tormenting cage: "De ces ongles il griffait la paroi dure de cette cage" ("With his nails he clawed the strong partition of this cage" [69]). The recurring plight of the traveler becomes that of the poet—he is condemned to immobility and stagnation while those around him, completely unaware of his misery, carry out their daily activities. Representing the contrast, the line, "Il était prisonnier du cauchemar ou de ses ennemis" ("He was prisoner of the nightmare or of his enemies"), is in opposition to "On marchait au dehors" ("One was walking outside"). As the nightmare abruptly ends, the poet awakens to sources of freedom and movement—"Et sa poitrine libre respirait un air frais qui changeait le décor" ("And his free chest was breathing a fresh refrain which changed the decor"). However, although the poet is outwardly free to come and go at will, inwardly he remains a prisoner to the haunting nightmare which is certain to recur: "Mais, dans sa mémoire persiste un mauvais souvenir" ("But, in his memory there persists a bad recollection").

Disorder and torment increase to the point where, in the poetry after 1928, one nightmare follows another. The themes of deterioration and death have already begun to obsess Reverdy in a final poem from *La Balle au bond,* "Pour mourir" ("To Die"). The demise of day foreshadows that of the poet. The natural surroundings are immobile, deserted, and decaying: "Il ne passera plus personne. La campagne est muette. Les pierres sèches. Un mur détruit. Le silence reprend" ("No one will pass by again. The countryside is mute. The stones dry. A destroyed wall. Silence is regained" [74]). Against the stillness of the natural world the only sign of life is death—"Un oiseau s'enfonce dans l'herbe pour mourir" ("A bird sinks into the grass to die").

II   *Prose: New Directions*

In contradistinction to the poetry written during the period 1921–1928, Reverdy's prose reveals a great variety in mood and genre, in addition to frequent evidence of the influence of his religious experience. A great deal of the prose from these years consists of short stories, many of which were written earlier, coinciding with the works *Cale sèche, Poèmes en prose* (1915); *Quelques poèmes, La Lucarne ovale* (1916); *Nord-Sud, Le Voleur de Talan* (1917); *Les Ardoises du toit, Les Jockeys camouflés* (1918); *La Guitare endormie, Self defence* (1919). One such example is the collection of short stories, *Risques et périls (Risks and Dangers)*, published in 1930, but written during the years 1915–1928. Beginning in 1917 and continuing until 1922, Reverdy composed *La Peau de l'homme (Man's Skin)*, another collection of short stories accompanied by a brief novel. These two collections represent Reverdy's first and only efforts at the genres in question. In addition, a work of aphorisms, *Le Gant de crin (Glove of Horsehair)* was published in 1927. Also containing aesthetics, this volume further clarified Reverdy's image theory and discussed the poet's ideas concerning the artist and his craft, as well as his religious feelings. Throughout these three works there are moments of light humor, confusion and disorder, religious ecstasy, and especially at the conclusion of the period, severe depression.

A.   Risques et périls *and* La Peau de l'homme

"Comment vivre dans cette rigoureuse et implacable incertitude?" ("How to live in this rigorous and unrelenting uncertainty?" [5]). Such is the general mood of dissatisfaction which permeates *Risques et périls* (*Risks and Dangers*),[9] ranging from ironical humor, the mildest form of protest, to bitter disappointment and tormenting visions. The earlier stories of this collection are written in poetic prose with no punctuation and varying margination. These include: "Les Amants réguliers" ("Steady Lovers") and "La Conversion" ("The Conversion"), both of 1915; "Les Hommes inconnus" ("Unknown Men") and "Le Passant bleu" ("The Blue Passer-by"), both published in 1919; and "Le Hachischin" ("The Hashish Taker") and "Le Buveur solitaire" ("The Solitary Drinker"), both published in 1922. Of the three remaining stories, published between 1926 and 1928, two, "La Poésie reine du vide et de l'art mordu" ("Poetry Queen of the Void and of Tormented Art") and "Maison hantée" ("Haunted House"), are written in conventional punctuated prose with a uniform left-hand margin, while one, "La Place dangereuse" ("The Dangerous Place" or "Square") is composed in a more liberal style, that is, with varied margination interspersed. Among the familiar, recurring poetic figures from Reverdy's first collections which are here represented are those of the wall, and the whirlwind, together with the themes of the voyage and void. The two former figures are, however, of only minor importance throughout *Risques et périls,* as is the theme of movement. In contrast are the two latter themes, which in addition to Reverdy's obsessions with religious skepticism and nightmares form the basic content of several of the later stories.

A statement from the opening story of *Risques et périls* explains perhaps why the poet has composed an entire series of short stories focusing upon the need for evasion, through religion as well as through art: "Le monde s'est plié en deux sous le poids de ce terrible ennui . . ." ("The world has folded in two under the weight of this terrible boredom . . ." [59]). Dissatisfaction with daily routine and unsuccessful encounters with other people, already depicted throughout Reverdy's early poems, drive him to seek other spheres of activity which, in conjunction with dream and self-analysis, are potentially conducive to self-fulfillment. The artist or the priest must assume the risk (hence the title *Risques et périls*) that creativity will be found lacking, or that spiritual strength will falter, but the energy involved in the attempt itself will at least contribute to inner density.

There is great variety of tone in the stories of *Risques et périls.* Reserved detachment in "La Conversion" is progressively modified so that in some stories such as "Le Hachischin" ("The Hashish Taker"), the reader is addressed in a vein of light humor juxtaposed with tones of fright and terror from haunting visions. Then in the final and longest text of the collection, "Maison hantée" ("Haunted House"), written at Solesmes after Reverdy's religious crisis, the theme of nightmare completely dominates the entire first portion. Series of tormenting scenes follow, each emphasizing distrust and hatred among men—

Les hommes décharnés se mordent sous le ciel humide, couvert des lourdes moisissures des saisons pourries. . . . Les hommes grouillent dans le brouillard étouffant du néant, l'édredon obsédant de la mort. . . . La haine a dessiné d'une pointe incisive le dos de l'homme dans la nuit.

Fleshless men bite one another under the humid sky, covered with heavy mildew from decayed seasons. . . . The men are swarming in the suffocating fog of nothingness, the haunting eiderdown of death. . . . Hatred has sketched with a cutting point man's back in the night. (127–28)

The movement of the sea here again connotes a destructive process, undermining whatever human efforts exist to make a new life—

. . . le bon sens rongé au-dessous du niveau de flottaison et les aspérités de la fantaisie émoussées par les perpétuels coups de langue des vagues, souillées par l'écume, éteintes par l'intarissable clapotis. . . .

. . . good sense consumed under the waterline mark and the sharpness of fantasy blunted by endless blows from the tongue of the waves, soiled by foam, extinguished by the inexhaustible lapping. . . . (129)

To the degradation enacted by the waves is joined the destructive force of the whirlwind, previously associated in Reverdy's poetry with the abyss and the void: " . . . à la suite de ces tourbillons d'eau gluante" (" . . . following these whirlwinds of gummy water"). Death, however, remains the ultimate result: "Cette troupe sinistre qui s'avance béatement vers la mort" ("This sinister band which advances contentedly toward death").

Other stories in this collection focus upon the search for self-identity, such as the earlier "Le Buveur solitaire" ("The Solitary Drinker"), but it is in "Maison hantée" where this theme receives the most emphasis. Yet, efforts to discern the function or purpose of a given human life are largely unsuccessful. Boundaries of severe restriction—a cell the perimeters of which are defined by a windowpane subjected to the

deleterious effects of the rain and wind, together with gates and bars
of fire—limit communication with the world of everyday reality as
well as with the more creative, intellectual reality of the imagination.
As if summarizing explicitly what he has so often confided through
implication in previous poems, Reverdy states that man's only certainty seems to be aimless wayfaring: "Où vas-tu malheureux vagabond de l'espace?" ("Where are you going, unfortunate vagabond of
space?" [132]).

At the conclusion of this introductory nightmare, the structure of the
text begins to resemble that of a maze, as one tormenting vision is
intermingled with another, each more eerie and fantastic. The poet
relates a spectral journey undertaken with a companion, Despair, during the course of which spirits narrate still another adventure. An
atmosphere of dread and misery is depicted as crimes are committed
and guilt shed. Finally, when the narrator seems to have reached the
end of this particular journey of ghoulish fantasy, he describes its
cathartic effect:

. . . je suis enfin sorti de la période de désespoir. J'ai guéri la tête, lavé l'esprit.
. . . je peux regarder droit devant moi sans glisser dans le vide immense où
tourne le vent qui vous entraîne. . . . et je peux marcher sans crainte de ren-
contrer cet immuable mur.

. . . I have finally gotten out of the period of despair. I have cured my head,
washed my spirit. . . . I can look straight in front of myself without slipping
into the immense void where the wind turns which carries you away. . . . and
I can walk without fear of meeting this immutable wall. (186–87)

Wandering aimlessly from one nightmare to another, he sees himself
existing only in terms of frail fragments, isolated from any possible
center of orientation. Elements of the setting progressively vanish until,
ultimately, only the narrator remains. All journeys have ended; all
efforts to escape the haunting present have proven futile: " . . . sa
décevante randonnée dans l'autre monde" (" . . . his disappointing cir-
cuit in the other world" [209]).

Tormenting visions appear to a much lesser extent in Reverdy's second collection of short stories, La Peau de l'homme.[10] The poet's attitude has changed somewhat, for in several texts a mood of resignation
has replaced that of acrid protest. The theme of evasion through dream
and memory continues, yet there is more of an emphasis upon movement, especially the force of the wind. Of the ten pieces in the collec-

tion, three are written in a poetic prose which alternates between a punctuated form and an unpunctuated form: "L'Imperméable" ("The Raincoat," 1916–1917); "Mirage" ("Mirage," 1917); and "Période Hors-texte" ("Period Outside the Text," 1918). Written soon after in poetic prose and also with varying margination are "La Maison seule" ("The House Alone") and "Ma pièce" ("My Room"), both published in 1919, and "Médaille neuve" ("New Medal"), published at approximately the same time. The remaining four texts are composed in classic prose style: "Une nuit dans la plaine" ("A Night in the Plain," 1917); and "La Peau de l'homme" ("Man's Skin"), "Au bord de l'ombre" ("At the Edge of Shadow"), and "Le Dialogue secret" ("Secret Dialogue"), all published about the year 1922. Among these last four pieces, "La Peau de l'homme" and "Le Dialogue secret"are to be given particular attention. The former represents Reverdy's first and only attempt at the novel, being—as he described it—"un roman populaire" ("a novel of the people"). The latter text, "Le Dialogue secret," one of the last texts written in this collection, anticipates the ghoulish scenes of the later "Maison hantée" (1928) in *Risques et périls*.

An early text of the collection *La Peau de l'homme*, "Période hors-texte" traces through dream and memory the poet's recollections of a past preceding the advent of his literary career. Published at about the same time as *Les Ardoises du toit* and *Les Jockeys camouflés* (both 1918), the text is a narration in poetic prose, combining several themes present in Reverdy's poetry at that time: restriction of movement, the voyage, reconstruction of the past, effacement, and finally, the void The entire text is structured around a voyage made by the narrator which at times is presented not so much in terms of movement as in terms of attempted absence. The narrator here, as so often in his poetry, perpetually seeks to be elsewhere:

> J'aurai passé la plus grande partie du
> temps hors de moi-même
> C'est comme une perpétuelle absence
> Une maladie

> I will have spent the most
> time outside of myself
> It is like a perpetual absence
> A disease

(137)

In contrast with the stagnant present is the reverse movement into
the past, a moment reconstructed around the lines of a house that had
apparently once belonged to the poet. The reconstructed moment,
however, crumbles. Where the house once stood, strangers now walk
among the ruins. As a scene closes, the prevailing effect is one of effacement through distance and wind force: "Ce n'est plus moi qui siffle au
fond du couloir. C'est le vent; le vide, l'ennui. C'est tellement loin
..." ("It is no longer I who whistle at the end of the corridor. It is the
wind; void, boredom. It is so far ..." [144]). The setting is also
destroyed by rupture and fragmentation: "Je suis au creux de la terre
qui se disloque" ("I am in the hollow of the earth which is breaking
up" [146]). Several other visions follow, and suddenly the narrator
awakens in a hospital bed. Another journey through dream begins,
again without transition; however, the familiar scene of the traveler
passing alone along a road gradually fades, effaced once again by the
wind.

Reverdy's attitude is more positive in the principal text of this collection, "La Peau de l'homme," a novel composed about four years
after "Période hors-texte." The work is intended as a portrait of Reverdy's close friend Picasso who appears first as a young boxer dependent upon the public's attention and approval, and then as a struggling
poet desirous of only pleasing his muse.[11] Tracing the early career of
the young man in Paris, the first portion of the story relates the events
of his education and early success in a world shaped by the dictates of
the public. The lighthearted tone of the narrative changes somewhat
as the reader learns that the well-educated man now begins to regret
having abandoned the classical studies of his youth. Although
extremely successful, he has chosen a surer, more facile method of
advancement, that of financial reward only: "Il a compris que ... il
était indispensable de se tourner vers cette foule avide, de la flatter ou
encore, en la dominant par l'intérêt, de la servir" ("He understood that
... it was essential to turn toward this greedy crowd, to flatter it or
even yet, by dominating it with interest, to serve it" [39]).

The second portion of this brief novel describes the feelings of
despair and discontent which torment the young man who now realizes
he has made a tragic mistake. He would have preferred a career of
more intellectual rewards, namely, poetry. Determined not to abandon
intellectual pursuits, the young boxer returns to poetic composition and
happily finds some success at selling his manuscripts. However, his
resentment against global indifference to art continues to grow until he
decides to take revenge. With an ending of tragic humor, the novel

terminates in a scene of destruction wrought by the boxer/poet. No longer controlling his great force, the young boxer, while supposedly training, begins to destroy parts of the city—houses shake, the banks of the Seine overflow, windows crack, cathedral stones break loose. Finally, the worst—the young man hits the sun with such strength that he extinguishes its light, and all its life-sustaining powers. A morbid peace follows or, in other words, the silence of the dead.

A similar ending is also found in what is probably the last text of *La Peau de l'homme*. Beginning as a dialogue between two travelers during the course of a voyage, the text "Le Dialogue secret" relives their dreams and nightmares. The attitude of the travelers becomes more and more skeptical as they visualize their likely fate—like pebbles thrown into a bag, they will be tossed about with countless other faces according to divine whims. God's negligence, already encountered in "Détresse du sort" (*Grande nature*) and in "Le Temps passe" (*La Balle au bond*), becomes particularly interesting in view of the probability that the dialogue was written just after Reverdy's conversion in 1921. In addition to divine indifference, the travelers feel they have no affinities with their fellowmen—"Je n'ai rien reconnu qui me ressemblât vraiment dans la forme de ces autres hommes" ("I recognized nothing in the form of these other men which truly resembled me" [195–96]). As the dialogue closes, they resign themselves to the fast-approaching, ineluctable end of the journey where they will take their place beside other anonymous bodies in a silent corner of the universe.

B. Le Gant de crin

When compared with the conflicting tones found in the prose of the years 1921–1928, *Le Gant de crin* (*Glove of Horsehair*) represents a brief period of resolution for Reverdy. There is a noticeable absence of the juxtaposed extremes of humor and depression, religious belief and skepticism. Written before and just after the retreat to Solesmes, *Le Gant de crin* reveals a unified spirit which has reached inner stability, both psychological and creative, through religious mysticism and art. It is a collection of aphorisms or observations relating to various aspects of art and creativity, the problems of the poet as an artist and as a man, and finally, Reverdy's religious beliefs, all of which are set forth in an extremely exhortative tone, especially the last section. It is, perhaps, Reverdy's only literary undertaking in which the resolution of interior conflict is absolute.

For Reverdy, the depth of dream is the richest source of poetic inspiration. The point of departure from which the poet begins his creative quest is the edge of a precipice: "Mais, s'il s'agit de poésie, où irons-nous chercher sa précieuse et rare matière si ce n'est aux bords vertigineux du précipice?" ("But, if it is a question of poetry, where will we go to look for its precious and rare material if it is not at the vertiginous edges of the precipice?" [17]). The descent from the precipice is synonymous with the poet's entry into an abyss, but it is not the haunting pit described in Reverdy's poetry. The abyss is, instead, a positive location, for it is here that the poet will yield to his imagination and sense impressions which will exploit the potential treasures of inspiration:[12] "Le rêve du poète, c'est l'immense filet aux mailles innombrables qui drague sans espoir les eaux profondes à la recherche d'un problématique trésor" ("The poet's dream is the immense net with numerous meshes which sweeps without hope the deep waters in the search for a dubious treasure").[13]

To dream is to flee ("Rêver, c'est fuir" [22]). The dream is seen as a refuge into which the mind can withdraw, thus avoiding all contact with the world of everyday existence. The world of dream knows no constraints; there, pure imagination flows uncontrolled, shaping the whims and fancies of the dreamer. Dividing dream into two aspects, Reverdy speaks of gratuitous dream and productive imagination. The former pursues no given objective, while the latter is directed by will ("la volonté"), the selective process of thought. Under such direction, imagination is no longer dream but instead the beginning of a creative project (24–25).

The process of creation is dependent, then, upon transformation occurring within several interrelated spheres. Poetic change occurs first at the intersection of dream and reality ("le rêve" and "la réalité" [18–19]).[14] Reality refers first to material objectivity, the everyday world dominated by sensory perceptions. It is here that man in the Pascalian tradition is thrown out like debris, *une épave*, condemned for the present to make his existence meaningful while immersed in an alien environment. His future is likewise doomed, for he can only anticipate death. However, Reverdy also speaks of deep reality ("la réalité profonde"), a realm located above the sphere of the concrete world and dominated by the infallible mind ("l'esprit"): "C'est l'esprit qui, au delà de l'apparence qui arrête le sens, pénètre librement, jusqu'au réel, l'essence des choses" ("It is the mind which, beyond appearance which stops the senses, penetrates freely, to the real, the essence of things"

[40]). It is in this new plane of existence, often called the real ("le réel"), that creation is realized. Having passed through the world of material objectivity and that of dream, the mind shapes the crystals of imminent poems (19).[15] The motion downward into dream and then upward into deep reality is reminiscent of the cycle descent/ascent of Rimbaud and Mallarmé. For Reverdy, dream leads down into a mine where he selects the best form of raw material which, upon ascension, will be transformed into perfect crystals: " . . . —mais de les remonter au jour sous forme de lingots, sous forme de bijoux" (" . . . —but to bring them back up to light in the form of bullion, of jewels" [23]).[16] In spite of the potentially infinite treasures of the dream, and the intellectual refinement of deep reality, the poet may be tempted by sensory gratification in the everyday world. Yet, however generous rewards may seem, this sphere of existence in fact offers the artist only uncertainty and solitude: "—Cette marche incertaine et précaire sur le vide, aspiré par en haut, attiré par en bas . . ." ("—This uncertain and precarious step upon the void, aspired from above, attracted from below . . ." [19]).

The process of poetic creation depends upon transformation, both in terms of successive locations and with regard to the role of the artist. However, in *Le Gant de crin* Reverdy emphasizes the static quality of the realized poem—" . . . ce qui est constant et permanent . . ." (" . . . what is constant and permanent . . ." [40])—and de-emphasizes in a manner reminiscent of the cubists, those aspects which are subject to change—" . . . ce qui n'est qu'apparent et fortuit, superficiel et accidentel" (" . . . what is only apparent and fortuitous, superficial, and accidental"). Accordingly, it is the static quality of art which places it in the realm of deep reality. Supporting the idea of constancy and permanence is the term *equilibrium*. A work of art is "un équilibre de forces, de forme, de valeurs, d'idées, de lignes, d'images, de couleurs" ("an equilibrium of forces, form, values, ideas, lines, images, colors" [46]) which opposes "le déséquilibre du mouvement" ("the imbalance of movement"). The artist must respect the limits of balanced structure, for static art is durable, lasting art (37).[17] In spite of Reverdy's preference for balance and constancy, his poetry written between 1913 and 1926 cannot generally be classified as static, but rather should be described as more static than his subsequent poetry. In opposition to many of his early poems where figures such as the crossroads or the wall imply indecision, immobility, or neutrality, numerous other poems of this same period are completely dominated by images of movement: rapid journeys along the horizon, cyclical transformation of day into night, changes in the focal point of a particular poem. The dichotomy between Reverdy's aesthetics and his creative work is only temporary; later, after 1930, his aesthetic writings will bear witness to the successive crises he experienced.

Another fundamental aspect of Reverdy's aesthetics discussed in *Le Gant de crin* is his image theory, initially revealed in *Nord-Sud*. The relevant passage in *Le Gant de crin* is a restatement of the earlier theory of confrontation between two more or less distant terms (30–31).[18] André Breton had by now already published his first surrealist manifesto (*Manifeste du surréalisme*) which quoted Reverdy's theory and explicated existing differences between it and his own beliefs. By repeating his ideas in *Le Gant de crin*, Reverdy emphasizes his differences with Breton.

Given the surrealist preoccupation with elements which were diametrically opposed, it is not surprising that Breton accorded great importance to Reverdy's theory.[19] However, Breton found it false to assume that the mind had consciously grasped the relationship between the two confronted realities. The emotive power of the image, according to Breton, was derived from a fortuitous confrontation which in turn produced the light of the image ("lumière de l'image"), the mind being restricted during the entire process to merely becoming aware of, and appreciating, the resultant spark [51]. Rejecting will and conscience ("la volonté" and "la conscience"), Breton preferred the "fortuitous" and the "arbitrary" ("le fortuit" and "l'arbitraire").[20] For Reverdy, the image had to be submitted to the censorship of the mind, while according to the surrealists, it was precisely this element of logical control which sterilized many of Reverdy's poems.[21]

Other points of disagreement soon become apparent. In addition to refusing to make linguistic expression subservient to logical thought, Breton espoused the use of automatic writing, a technique not favored by Reverdy. Believing that the speed of thinking was inferior to that of linguistic expression, Breton supported creativity through dialogue between the conscious and subconscious during which the artist noted on paper everything that came into his head with no preconceived thoughts or exterior influences whatsoever.[22]

Reverdy's notes on aesthetics form only a minor portion of *Le Gant de crin*, the remaining, lengthier sections describing the apex of the artist's spiritual evolution. Of the three degrees of "interior life"

(dream, thought, and contemplation) which the poet enumerated at
the beginning of *Le Gant de crin*, in the second half of this work he
is preoccupied only with the last. Complete liberty of thought could
only be found in total submission to, and effacement before, God.[23]
Inspiration and its resultant creation no longer represent the highest
good for Reverdy; it is rather complete immersement in the worship
of God.[24]

Never again would Reverdy's religious beliefs reach such a degree
of total acceptance and unlimited faith. Reverdy confides that it was
through art that he came initially to know God: the moment of contact
between the human soul and the raw poetic material is a divine gift.
It is an illusion to believe that man can individually achieve unity and
understanding among fellowmen; true brotherhood can only be realized through God:

. . . nous nous apercevons que l'union parfaite et totale entre les hommes est
impossible. Nous nous heurtons à un mur de glace. Il y a un trou noir qui
nous paraît être le plus profond de nous-même, et qui, pourtant, nous est
étranger à nous-même.

. . . we perceive that perfect and total union among men is impossible. We
run into a wall of glass. There is a black hole which appears to us to be the
deepest of ourselves, and which, however, is alien even to ourselves.[25]

Images of isolation now come to mind—the ubiquitous wall and its
counterparts—the eyelid, room, partitions, gates, riverbanks; outlines
of objects, and in addition, references to separation—the pit or abyss,
mirror, and crossroads. Complete self-knowledge is impossible; it is
indeed the domain of God. Accordingly, each individual must bring
himself to God, and through divine love will realize universal com-
munion. Quoting Baudelaire, Reverdy states, "'Tout est commun entre
les hommes, *même* Dieu.' C'est *surtout* Dieu qu'il fallait dire"
("'Everything is common among men, *even* God.' It is *especially* God
that he should have said").[26] God is infinitely good, merciful, just, and
pure (107). Referring to the title of this particular work, Reverdy suggests that any seemingly harsh action by God is well-deserved: "La
main de Dieu nous paraît souvent rude parce qu'il traite ses amis
débiles avec un gant de crin" ("The hand of God often appears harsh
to us because He treats His weak friends with a glove of horsehair"

[75]). Even death, which would come to haunt Reverdy unremittingly after *Le Gant de crin,* appears in a positive light, for deceived by everyday superficialities, man with sufficient faith can realize spiritual happiness in the supernatural and invisible world of the departed (135–36).

CHAPTER 5

Severe Depression and Psychological Upheaval

THE short-lived moment of reassuring calm captured in *Le Gant de crin* is no longer apparent in most of Reverdy's work after 1928. The torment and unrest which the poet had voiced intermittently, now erupted into a torrent of disillusion. The origins of Reverdy's unrest are enumerated in the collection *Sources du vent* (*Sources of the Wind*, 1929), where the wind, usually a negative figure in Reverdy's poetry, connotes incoherent contrast between intense, destructive movement and an abrupt suspension of all motion. Included in this work and in *Pierres blanches* (*White Stones*) which appeared the following year, are the themes of violent dispersal, shipwreck, death, and effacement, juxtaposed with a state of complete neutralization. When the wind is not the agent of destruction, the accusing finger points directly to God who, having finished his creation, has now abandoned it, as in the collection *Flaques de verre*. The turbulence of liquid passage in this last work is further explicated in the final work of the chapter, *Le Livre de mon bord* (*My Journal*), in which human presence appears in the form of debris as the poet becomes resigned to the utter meaninglessness of life. If the poet's journal does admit one element of certainty, it is that the ongoing process of disintegration is paradoxically one of permanence and continuity.

I   *Increasing Hostility and Unpredictable Change*

A.   Sources du vent *and* Pierres blanches

Sources du vent,[1] composed with varied margination, is Reverdy's largest collection. Although much of this poetry repeats descriptions of natural cycles included earlier in *La Balle au bond*, the more original poems foreshadow the violent movement and absence of control so

119

prevalent in *Ferraille*, the climactic work of Reverdy's psychological torments. Yet an uncontrollable, spectral immobility counters the haunting fears of destructive movement, not only in *Sources du vent*, but also in a shorter collection, *Pierres blanches*. Immobility, although not an agent of active destruction, produces a neutralizing effect, that is, eternally prolonging a state of transition or even transforming such a state of suspense into finalized paralysis.

The introductory poem of *Sources du vent*, "Chemin tournant" ("Winding Path"), is a statement of Reverdy's dissatisfaction with life. The specter of death quietly awaits its moment: "Il y a un terrible gris de poussière dans le temps" ("There is a terrible grey dust in time" [81]; "Un goût de cendre sur la langue" ("A taste of ashes on the tongue"). Permeating the entire first stanza, is the force of the wind, Reverdy's ubiquituous harbinger of ill things; stirring up the waters, it initiates the turning, twisting motion connoted in the title "Chemin tournant": "Les échos sourds de l'eau dans le soir chavirant" ("Deaf echoes of the water in the capsizing night"). The verb *chavirer* prepares the reader for a further line, "Le navire du coeur qui tangue" ("The ship of the heart which pitches"). The action of the verbs *chavirer* and *tanguer* implies abrupt changes of setting, rapid succession of scenes, none of which seems to have brought the poet what he was looking for.

The moment of reversal becomes more violent as the lashing force of the wind intensifies. Often, as in the text "Paysage à bêtes" ("Countryside With Animals"), the destruction of the wind is associated with the arrival of day. A tone of sorrow is established preceding dawn's burst of light—dead flowers, tears, remorse, grooves of earth, and finally, the abyss. The brightness of dawn creates the effect of a conflagration and suddenly, the image of the ship pitching and capsizing is repeated: "Tout tourne sur la terre plate qui chavire" ("Everything turns on the flat earth which capsizes" [96]).

If the present only constitutes disillusionment and incoherent dispersal, the past offers no possibility for escape. Once again in the poem "Galeries" ("Galleries") a nocturnal setting unfurls twisted and misshapen by the force of the wind: "Un entonnoir immense où se tordait la nuit/Des lambeaux s'échappaient par moments" ("An immense funnel where night was twisting/Shreds escaped by moments" [125]). The term *entonnoir* is here a synonym for the whirlwind or *tourbillon* of earlier collections such as *La Lucarne ovale* and *Les Ardoises du toit*. As with the text "Paysage à bêtes," the coming of night is not accompanied by measure and control, the term *lambeaux* in this latter poem heightening the effect of the uncontrollable vortex. The poet associates violent movement with the figure of the wall as he attempts to seek refuge in his past. The vibrations of the air awaken thoughts of a former life; rows of faces appear and form a temporal partition, further supported by a falling curtain: "On ne peut plus avancer/Toutes les portes sont fermées" ("One can no longer advance/All the doors are closed"). Although movement into the past is refused, the setting of the poem yields to the spinning rhythm of the funnel: "Le centre se déplace" ("The center is displaced" [126]). The inscrutability of life completely disarms the poet; as close as the past is, it remains in this poem forever inaccessible, and just as the poet attempts to confront the challenges of the present, that too escapes his grasp:

> La vie entière est en jeu
> Constamment
> Nous passons à côté du vide élégamment
> sans tomber
> Mais parfois quelque chose en nous fait tout trembler
> Et le monde n'existe plus

> Your complete life is at stake
> Constantly
> We pass beside the void elegantly
> without falling
> But sometimes something within us makes everything shake
> And the world no longer exists
>
> (126)

The immobility of the expressionless faces is repeated in that of the void, a neutralization of the effect of the vortex. Spinning out of control, such a whirlwind of conflicting torments has thrown itself into paralysis and disintegration.

Reverdy's interest in immobility is continued in several other texts of the collection where he returns to poetic figures used earlier in *Poèmes en prose* and *La Lucarne ovale*. The constant renewal of natural cycles is met with bewilderment and disbelief as the passersby in the poem "Au-delà" ("Beyond") grow weary of staring at what they cannot understand. Their complete detachment from the natural surroundings is reminiscent of the earlier collection *Grande nature*.[2] "Le Mur de pierres" ("Wall of Stones"), as the title indicates, is structured upon the figure of the wall. The barrier in this poem cannot be crossed or scaled, yet the poet refuses to relinquish his hope of success. If upward mobility is precluded, so is movement in the opposite direction: "En bas les femmes passaient une à une/Mais la porte s'est refermée" ("Below the women passed one by one/But the door has closed again" [162]). The poet and reader are suspended somewhere *between* the directions upward and downward; their position further heightens the effect of the door and wall, especially bringing to mind the texts of *Poèmes en prose* where the preposition "between" connotes restriction and confinement.

Elsewhere in the collection *Sources du vent*, a more pessimistic view preoccupies the poet. As night falls in the poem "Espace" ("Space"), light from a star is transferred to a writer's lamp, signifying creativity and renewal. In one quick movement, the chain can be pulled, the light extinguished; life can be forever destroyed:

L'étoile échappée
L'astre est dans la lampe
La main
tient la nuit
par un fil
Le ciel
s'est couché
contre les épines
Des gouttes de sang claquent sur le mur
Et le vent du soir
sort d'une poitrine

The star escaped
The star is in the lamp
The hand
holds night
by a string
The sky
has retired
against thorns
Drops of blood splatter against the wall
And the wind of evening
is exhaled from the breast
(224)

The lines are arranged to form a circle in the center, thereby graphically reproducing the void created when the chain is pulled. The bed of thorns and the splattering drops of blood connote the suffering and misery of unknown darkness. The wind in the final lines of the poem bears a positive connotation, signifying the fragility of the last breath of life, of the last spurt of inspiration.

The actual disappearance of the writer's creative *élan* is described in "Rien" ("Nothing"). Other elements of the setting—bells, lights, shreds of songs, birds, voices, even shadows and walls—appear and abruptly vanish from sight. "Rien" more specifically describes the poet's despair at the end of the poem "Espace": "Il n'y a même plus de place/Pour les mots que je laisserai" ("There is not even any more room/For the words which I will leave" [231]). The void paradoxically constitutes emptiness and filled space. All elements of the setting have disappeared. Yet there is no place for encouragement or interest in the artist's text.

The death theme—just now seen in the solitary cross, the images of blood and thorns, together with the effacement of setting and text—becomes more personal and intensely realistic in *Pierres blanches*.[3] Throughout the poem "Il devait en effet faire bien froid" ("It Was Indeed To Be Very Cold"), the poet describes with great contrast the hours of visitation following his own death. The familiar psychological context of the room as a setting of emotional reconciliation or of the union of past and present is transposed in this text to one of purely physical dimensions. It is more appropriately called a chamber, a funeral chamber. The contrasts between the *moi* and *je* and those visiting the chamber correlate with the extremes immobility/mobility, death/life. The *moi* is motionless while the chimes ring all at once, simultaneity and interaction being juxtaposed with solitude and immobility. Once again, Reverdy has used line to suggest death: "De la tapisserie où mon corps s'aplatit de/profil . . ." ("From the tapestry where my body lies in/profile . . ." [285]). Looking back upon his former life as a block in time, the *moi* understands that it, too, like himself, has been reduced to an object: " . . . je regarde ma vie d'où je me suis/retiré" (" . . . I look at my life from where I have/withdrawn").

Beginning the reconstruction of his previous life, the poet describes with terms of contradiction. The lines "Les distances sont abolies et pourtant tout reste/en place" ("The distances are abolished and however everything remains/in place") present the opposition of abrupt motion and a complete absence of change. Although distances have been dissolved, everything remains the same. The glacial funeral chamber of death is only replaced by that of life. In life as in death, there is no interaction, only separation. No specific shapes or character emerge; all that the deceased can resurrect are objects or memories of a certain material thickness.

B.   Flaques de verre

Published in 1929, the same year as *Sources du vent*, the collection *Flaques de verre* (*Pools of Glass*)[4] differs greatly in form and thematic material. Consisting of poetry written in punctuated prose, it departs from such conventional themes as the progression of natural cycles, so prevalent in *La Balle au bond* and *Sources du vent*, and instead depicts with infinitely more intensity the uncontrollable violence and disorder with which the poet was increasingly obsessed. Having abandoned the cubist preoccupation with the interrelationships of objects in a controlled, immobile space, Reverdy now sought the germ of poetry in abrupt, unpredictable change:

Et ce ciel, tourmenté et changeant, qui se reflète sur les routes, à peine dessinées, de l'avenir, dans les flaques, ce ciel qui attire nos mains, ce ciel soyeux, caressé tant de fois comme une étoffe—derrière les vitres brisées, la poésie, sans mots et sans idées, qui se découvre.

And this sky, tormented and changing, which is reflected upon the roads, scarcely drawn, of the future, in pools, this sky which attracts our hands, this silky sky, caressed so many times as a piece of fabric—behind the broken panes, poetry, without words or ideas, which discovers itself. (6)

The terms "tourmenté et changeant" in this introductory quotation of *Flaques de verre* especially indicate the poet's state of mind. Each vision is progressively transposed into pools of reflection, hence the title, and then each previously frozen image is shattered into involuntary dispersal.

As the title suggests, Reverdy gives much attention throughout the collection to the poetic figures of the storm and flood, together with the resultant destruction caused by uncontrollable liquid passage. Introduced earlier, the figure of the storm has been associated with nightmare and descent into the void in "Maison hantée" of *Risques et périls* and with abrupt changes of setting as in "Chemin tournant" and "Paysages à bêtes" from *Sources du vent*. The poem "Naufrages sans bouées" ("Shipwrecks Without Buoys") develops the theme of mankind seen as *épaves*, pieces of wreckage tossed about haphazardly. The poem centers around families who hope to be saved from rising flood waters. Rescue boats ply toward them, but ambiguity concerning the success of the outcome is maintained: "A quelque distance, il y a de profonds remous où les épaves dansent et l'escalier qui continue peut-être jusqu'au fond" ("At some distance there are deep eddies where flotsam dances and the stairway which continues perhaps to the bottom" [15]). The term *remous* recalls the whirlwind, this time in liquid form, and its spinning motion traces the spiral shape of the stairway. Descent into the depths of the spiral is equivalent to a fall into the void. When rescue proves to be impossible for everyone, those who remain are viewed as successors to the debris. They are rolled and washed about by the waves, and sinisterly caressed and preened for their death scene: " . . . tous ces coeurs désolés qui flottent au gré du sort et roulent sur le sable ondulé que les lames sournoises caressent dans le fond, lissent et peignent" (" . . . all those regretful hearts which float to the will of fate and roll along the undulating sand which the cunning waves deeply caress, preen, and comb" [16]).

Uncontrollable whirlpools may also relate to psychological torments. Reverdy introduces the text "Vitesse des mots" ("Speed of Words") with the expression "remous vertigineux de la prière" ("vertiginous eddies of prayer"); instead of providing orientation and a stabilized base of thought, they have only created further confusion and incoherence. Confronting the ineffectiveness of prayer, the poet relates the effect of his disappointment: "Les larmes glissent . . . les larmes en colliers ruisselants viennent alimenter les fleuves, au mouvement tragique, de la terre" ("Tears slip away . . . tears in streaming necklaces come to feed the rivers, in the tragic movement, of the earth" [118]). Uncontrolled liquid passage then produces complete incoherence: "Je me perds. Je cherche. Je me perds" ("I am losing myself. I am searching. I am losing myself" [120]). Traveling through confused visions, the poet finds that routes have been washed away, roads collapse; all reason seems to have been abandoned. Like the debris in "Naufrages sans bouées," the poet too is about to be swept into the force of the whirlpool: "Je descends, avec l'eau qui court, noyant mon ombre, vers la mer. Mais je ne sais déjà plus ce que je cherche . . ." ("I am descending, with the water which runs, drowning my shadow, toward the sea. But I no longer already know what I am seeking . . ." [120]). If he still has a purpose, it is perhaps to restore his lost inner peace and calm; yet, the success of this undertaking is perpetually in doubt. Just as in Reverdy's earlier poems (*Poèmes en prose* and *La Lucarne ovale*), the poet/voyager remains alone yet surrounded by unresponsive *others*. Emptiness is paradoxically occupied space, but meaninglessly occupied space. Elsewhere, in "Au Bord des terres" ("At the Edge of Lands"), extremes continue. The force of the wind brings all voyages to a standstill, yet shakes the shores, creating deadly undertows.

The theme of the storm and its destructive effects is treated more specifically as the poet associates it with the misery of its victims. In "Lumière dure" ("Harsh Light"), the poet's attitude is one of despair. The sight of an old woman crouching at a crossroads creates visions of bewildered people, tossed about whimsically by the wind: "Fantômes de l'esprit, êtres dépaysés, tourbillons que le vent soulève ..." ("Specters of the mind, bewildered beings, whirlwinds which the wind raises ..." [78]). It is again the figure of the wall which, as in "Galeries," confirms the absence of hope; it is endless and too high to be scaled. All attempts of those within the setting to counter the force of the wind stop just as they approach the barrier: " ... c'est devant un mur sans fin, ... que se tient cette femme perdue ..." (" ... it is in front of a wall without end, ... that this lost woman stands ...").

Although there is usually no explanation for the theme of violent, liquid passage in *Flaques de verre*, "Messager de la tyrannie" ("Messenger of Tyranny") and "L'Âme en péril" ("Soul in Peril") are exceptions. Both texts recall the theme of an uncaring superior force introduced earlier in "Entre deux mondes" and "Projets" of *Les Ardoises du toit*, and then later developed in "Détresse du sort" of *Grande nature*, "Le temps passe" of *La Balle au bond*, and "Le Dialogue secret" of *La Peau de l'homme*. Having introduced the poem "Messager de la tyrannie" with a series of sentences beginning with the personal pronoun *il*, Reverdy enumerates the violent deeds of an unidentified being. The action of flowing is especially emphasized: "Il crache des étincelles sur la nuit, de la cendre, de l'amour, des éclairs, des ailes cassées, de la haine, des étoiles et des pièces d'or qui s'éloignent. Il crache les soupirs du remords sur la nuit. ... Il lui enfonce le silence dans la gorge" ("He spits out sparks upon the night, ashes, love, flashes, broken wings, hatred, stars, and pieces of gold which move away. He spits out the sighs of remorse upon the night. ... He thrusts silence down his throat" [8]). All of the elements of a human life, most of which are negative, have been broken and dispersed. Never precisely identified, the force behind this destruction appears to be an insensate God or Supreme Being: "Tout est serré dans cette main qui jamais ne pardonne" ("Everything is grasped in this hand which never pardons"

[9]). The fate which awaits his kingdom, as stated here, is constant torment, a past consumed by hellfires, a present forever disintegrating. The text closes as it began, with an emphasis upon inundation, but this time the verb *ruisseler* has been substituted for *cracher:* "Il ne reste plus rien que la salive noire, ruisselant sur la nuit, et la haine, l'amour, l'or, le désir de l'or, la liberté sans ailes, la morsure contre les chaînes" ("There remains nothing more than black saliva, streaming upon the night, and hatred, love, gold, the desire for gold, liberty without wings, the biting against the chains"). The fragments of life which this God has mashed and ground now constitute the black liquid, blood possibly, and hence evil desire and impending death which surge into every cranny. The paradoxical permanence of disintegration is suggested in the chains and in the nonexistence of liberty: "la liberté sans ailes." Relentless in his desire for defilement, the vengeful designs of the God will not be compromised—he is " . . . la force qui pèse et qui tue, toute la force" (" . . . the force which weighs and which kills, the whole force" [9]).

Another poem of death, "Les Blancs déserts de l'immortalité de l'âme" ("The Deserted Voids of the Immortality of the Soul"), is centered upon a memory, a previous relationship of love between the poet and an unidentified person. Reference to the memory is made by the repetition of the terms "Il n'y a plus . . . entre l'amour et moi, que . . ." ("There is only . . . between love and myself . . ."), each substituted fragment connoting death: " . . . que les stigmates livides de la mort . . ." (" . . . only the livid stigmas of death . . ."); " . . . que l'étreinte glacée des poignées de mains rugueuses de l'angoisse" (" . . . only the icy grip of rough handshakes of anguish"); " . . . que les gouttes de sang qui tracent mon chemin dans les gorges de la défaite" (" . . . only drops of blood which trace my way into the gorges of defeat"). Those who inhabit this ruptured memory are deformed spirits, nameless and similarly nondescript: " . . . des personnages blancs, avec des visages blancs, des corps blancs, des tourments blancs, des remords presque blancs, des idées blanches; et moi qui deviens peu à peu, dans ce tourbillon sans portée, incolore" (" . . . white characters, with white faces, white bodies, white torments, remorse almost white, white ideas; and I myself who become colorless, little by little, in this whirlwind without bearing" [131–32]). The absence of detail and color is repeated in a description of the sea, where the incoherent whirlwind of death has been stilled: "La mer qui borde la plage vers le nord ne bouge pas. Les crêtes de ses vagues sont fermes et immobiles" ("The sea which borders the beach toward the north does not move. The crests of its waves are rigid and immobile" [132]). Yet, in spite of these poems of death, Reverdy at this time had not completely resigned himself to surrender. In the poem "La Tête pleine de beauté" ("Head Full of Beauty"), he describes the forces of contrast which taunt him, the motion which could alert his consciousness and summon his creative energies: "Vertigineuse pesée des forces ennemies. Chemins mêlés dans le fracas des chevelures. Toi, douceur et haine,—" ("Vertiginous strength of enemy forces. Paths mingled in the din of heads of hair. You, gentleness and hatred—" [135]). Indeed, in the concluding lines of the poem, the unpredictability of the moment is interpreted in a highly positive vein: "Toi, pureté, pivot éblouissant du flux et du reflux de ma pensée dans les lignes du monde" ("You, pureness, dazzling pivot of the ebb and flow of my thought in the lines of the world").

II   *The Reader Taken Into Confidence: Reflection and Outburst in* Le Livre de mon bord

The devastating unrest of *Flaques de verre* continues in *Le Livre de mon bord* (*My Journal*), yet at the same time this journal describing the artist's successive states of mind offers moments of reflection and meditation upon a multitude of subjects of greater variety than in the earlier *Le Gant de crin*. Composed as a collection of meditations, *Le Livre de mon bord* was written during the years 1930–1936, but not published until 1948. Written in a tone more personal and confiding than *Le Gant de crin*, this later work portrays Reverdy more as an observer than as an advisor, and comments upon language, human weaknesses, harsh realities such as the contrast of illusion and truth, incoherence, withdrawal; the eternal process of transformation and contradiction; death, as well as earlier subjects of aesthetics and religion. While *Le Gant de crin* treated some of Reverdy's aesthetic theories and religious beliefs, it did not directly relate these to the poet's recurring thematic material. However, this last work of extreme confidence in the reader departs from the earlier tone of isolation and, instead, describes themes of intense movement and psychological upheaval which had tormented the poet in prior works and which would appear in future collections such as *Ferraille* and *Le Chant des morts*. During the six-year period while Reverdy was composing *Le Livre de mon bord*, he published no further collections of poetry. Created as a moment of respite, it was an opportunity for him to reflect upon and digest prior moments of crisis before undertaking those of extreme rupture yet to come.

In a discussion of one of his principal themes, that of the voyage, Reverdy analyzes its attraction to the wayfarer. First, the opportunity to journey is a potential for change, a chance to alter the boredom and misery of indifference and neglect. Since the type of future change is unknown, there is an aura of mystery and intrigue which suggests possible communication with *others*, positive relationships breaking the traveler's conventional solitude. The mysterious quality of unexplored experiences appears in the form of smoke; smoke, rather than sails: "C'est la fumée qui nous attire ou nous pousse, et nous n'avons plus qu'un désir, un besoin, une angoisse—dévoiler" ("It is smoke which attracts us or propels us, and we have only one desire, one need, one care—to discover").[5] To learn the true nature of the smoke, to unveil the mystery is the traveler's constant goal. In addition, the journey represents a necessary illusion. Each departure is flight and each flight an appearance of being somewhere else. It is indeed the need to be somewhere else, the idea of departure which constitutes human hope. The transition between being in one place and the decision to leave is the true moment of change, which although illusory, offers the greatest potential for reformation:

Fuir et rester. Être—c'est être là, rien de plus—et, fuir, le besoin d'être ailleurs. Dans le moment où nous décidons de partir, nous ne sommes plus—ni là ni ailleurs, brève illusion, car être ailleurs c'est déjà, de nouveau, être enchaîné.

Fleeing and remaining. Being—it is being there, nothing more—and, fleeing, the need to be elsewhere. In the moment when we decide to leave, we are no longer—neither there nor elsewhere, brief illusion, for being elsewhere is already, once again, being enchained. (7)

Arriving, remaining, and departing all bear meaningless values.

Whether change actually occurs, whether a different result is effected in contrast to the status quo is not important; in that respect, human character may seem stationary. The idea of being elsewhere and the precious moments before making the final decision to leave constitute a perpetual source of transformation, paradoxically a guaranteed continuity which is true reality: " . . . c'est-à-dire qu'il n'y a rien de réel en soi mais un mouvement dont la perpétuelle continuité est la seule réalité" (" . . . that is to say that there is nothing real in and of itself but a movement of which perpetual continuity is the only reality" [191]).

There are other aspects of reality, however, to which adjustment is much more difficult. The poet's pessimism and severe depression, especially in *Flaques de verre*, *Ferraille*, and *Le Chant des morts*, were derived from successive disappointments; life had not measured up to the poet's expectations:

Le malheur est que pour bien connaître et comprendre la vie, il faut avoir appris beaucoup de désillusion de la vie et que le mépris de la mort ne va pas sans autant de mépris de la vie.

The misfortune is that to know and understand life well, it is necessary to have experienced much disillusion of life and that the contempt for death does not go without as much scorn for life. (157)

In how many poems has the reader sensed the isolation throughout the voyage, at the crossroads, along the horizon? Human selfishness and egotism have caused men to withdraw into themselves for solace. Reaching, grasping the mind of modern man is a false hope; he is now sad and stagnant (19). If somehow the hiatus in communication is bridged ("l'abîme de malentendus, de méconnaissance et d'incompréhension" [39]), this positive movement forward is also illusory; even the slightest line ("Une ligne imperceptible suffit, irréductible, infranchissable—"/"An unperceivable line suffices, irreducible, impassable" [39–40]) forms the most formidable barrier. In a tone more of resignation than of bitterness, Reverdy confides that because of hostility and distrust, true stability and inner peace can only be found within oneself. The wall which isolates and restricts also shelters and provides refuge. It was probably for this reason that Reverdy continued to live at Solesmes after his religious fervor had died.

One possible problem in human communication, as Reverdy observed, was the extremely narrow connotation which writers associated with particular terms. Words, for Reverdy, were to be free, completely detached from conventional meanings or preconceived contexts, as indeed he had recommended in *Self defence*. However, semantic freedom in *Le Livre de mon bord* seems to be more extensive, for Reverdy stresses the change in connotation the word may undergo at the hands of successive authors:

Les mots sont l'aile des idées, ils doivent les porter librement loin de toi, le plus loin possible de toi—les détacher de toi—les dépersonnaliser—elles vaudront d'autant plus qu'elles seront plus aux autres qu'à toi.

Words are the wing of ideas, they must carry them freely far from you, the farthest possible from you—they must detach them from you—depersonalize them—the ideas will have all the more value if they are worth more to others than just to you. (78)

However, the incoherence and meaninglessness of life, whether in a semantic or physical sense, has not plagued all men. Some have avoided isolation and indifference by a close relationship to God, but Reverdy excludes himself from this group. He preferred to seek the truth about God, about the sources of incoherence, about the abyss: "Mais, ce n'est pas la paix que je cherchais; seulement la vérité. J'étais excédé, obsédé par l'idée fixe, morbide du néant" ("But, it is not peace which I was seeking; only the truth. I was worn out, obsessed by the fixed and morbid idea of nothingness" [174]). Although Reverdy seems to imply that he never learned the truth about God's existence, he did determine that God and religion were two separate entities, the latter especially used as a pretext to avoid confronting the former. Laden with unnecessary trappings and decorations, a religious sect diverted attention from the true subject of adoration, thereby creating potentially insurmountable problems in the knowledge of the divine. The sources for life's incoherence, along with its unpredictable change and upheaval—the overflowing void, the descent into the pit, the aimless wandering of the wayfarer, the circular spiral, the destructive whirlwind—are not enumerated; Reverdy prefers to resign himself to this state of meaninglessness from whence he came, hence the image of the *épave*, and where he will continue to flounder: "Aujourd'hui, confus est l'état où nous sommes, comme l'était celui d'où nous sortons, et confus celui vers lequel nous allons . . ." ("Today, confused is the state where we are, as was that from which we come, and confused that toward which we are going . . ." [205]).

Although for Reverdy there seemed little that was certain, his exploration of the abyss was perhaps more successful. Associated with death and eventual disintegration, the abyss was the traveler's final destination, toward which he would drift helplessly, like the *épave*. The moment of transition in the earthly voyage, a source of comfort for the poet, became in the fatal descent a moment of terror: "Il est vrai que

je pensais surtout à l'horrible moment de transition. Ce passage répug-
nant de la forme à l'informe, cet effroyable glissement de l'être phy-
sique au néant" ("It is true that I was especially thinking of the horrible
moment of transition. This repugnant passage of form to formless, this
frightful slipping of physical being to nothingness" [175]). Death, for
Reverdy, was hideous; it was a perpetual nightmare of all that was
elongated, rigid, cold, forever silent (174). Although he encountered it
in his memories, dreams, and daily fantasies, he never became accus-
tomed to the reality of the ultimate voyage downward.

CHAPTER 6

Self-Devastation: Ferraille

THE numerous psychological crises which had plagued Reverdy culminated in countless descriptions filling the pages of *Ferraille* *(Scrap Iron).*[1] A collection of twenty-six poems, only two of which are written in punctuated poetic prose, *Ferraille* is dominated by dreams and visions narrated in the first person singular, the *je* in effect recounting self-destruction by the liquid obliteration of mind, memory, and spirit. In this collection Reverdy returns to formal stanzas and meters, and for the most part, a traditional uniform left-hand margin. Gone are the semantically significant white spaces, replaced by the more formal, somber *verset*. The title itself, *Ferraille* or *Scrap Iron*, suggests fragments or again, the *épaves*, flotsam remaining from previous shipwrecks, from earlier rupture and dispersal. Published in 1937, one year after the completion of *Le Livre de mon bord, Ferraille* indicates that the poet's partial literary silence had ended, giving way to stored-up fears of torment and deprivation. The deviant liquid state now realizes the process of decay and deterioration alluded to earlier, especially in *Flaques de verre.*

Frequently associated with violent liquid passage in *Ferraille* is the theme of the voyage, during which fears of destruction and death are created by flood tides and surging waves, together with the deadly undertow of blood flowing through arteries and veins. The action of fleeing and the state of remaining after having once arrived continue as in *Le Livre de mon bord* to offer no hope of positive change; it is still the idea of being elsewhere and the mystery of those few transitional moments prior to the decision to flee which encourage the wayfarer toward therapeutic transformation. The composition of the sea and rivers along which the voyage occurs changes in *Ferraille*. Whether water or blood, the liquid now contains negative elements such as venoms and scum as in "Les Buveurs d'horizons" ("Drinkers

133

of the Horizons"). In this poem those who have just arrived from their journey are no happier, reminiscent of Baudelairian discontent:

> Ils rentrent dans le creux des bouges
> Ils se cachent
> Et l'exil et le spleen et l'ennui se partagent
> leur coeur et leur esprit. . . .
>
> They return to the hollows of slums
> They hide themselves
> And exile and spleen and boredom eat at
> their heart and spirit. . . .
>
> (338)

Their once fervent ardor now ferments and grows rancid; yet, they still retain the hope of leaving: "Ce soir l'esprit troublé du goût irritant de partir" ("Tonight the spirit troubled by the irritating taste to leave" [339]). This journey will perhaps unravel the past, not only that of the poet but also the past of *others* who, too, are all caught up in the incoherence that is life. Water and the sea are now transposed into blood as the poet's depression becomes that of the world:

> Ivresse du sang mêlé
> De la détresse de mon coeur et de mon corps
> Au monde entier
>
> Drunkeness of mixed blood
> Of the anguish of my heart and of my body
> To the entire world
>
> (339)

The journey through raging flood waters continues to be associated with the figures of the whirlwind and the abyss. The poem "Sur la ligne" ("On the Line") depicts the traveler succumbing to fatigue and subject to the force of the wind upon the sea: "Fatigue des élans trop creux de ta mâture/Dégoût du sang trop lourd qui bouleverse ta figure" ("Fatigue of too hollow outbursts of the masts/Distaste for blood too heavy which upsets your face" [370]). The sea of blood capsizes the boat as indeed it does the poet's inner stability, and in a reverse movement forms swirls which funnel into the pit: "Et le recul nocturne qui tourbillonne au gouffre" ("And the nocturnal movement backward which swirls to the abyss"). No longer in control of his direction, the wayfarer again assumes the role of *épave,* a victim of physical and psychological shipwreck, bound for certain death: "Seul sur le roc glissant des fièvres de la mort" ("Alone upon the rock slipping from the fevers of death").

In other poems of *Ferraille,* the role of the poet is extremely active, suggesting open revolt even if there is no real hope of success. The poem "Les Battements du coeur" ("Heartbeats") again recounts a voyage upon a sea of blood, but this time, the journey is an interior one; the boat is driven through arteries by pulsations, rather than the ocean's waves. Noting the resemblance between a human body in poor health, perhaps his own, and a machine in disrepair, Reverdy hopes to achieve through the journey a rebirth or rejuvenation: "On remettra peut-être enfin la mécanique en mar/che..." ("At last one will perhaps put the mechanism back into/service" [368]). The blood, pausing as it builds up its strength, is likened to the sea which also regulates the passage of its waves: "Où le sang trop léger reconstitue ses vagues/ Quand la houle pousse à grands coups d'épaule sur/le bord" ("Where the blood too light builds up its waves/When the swell pushes with great effort upon/the edge" [368]). In spite of the poet's determination to effect positive change, he knows that the voyage is only an illusion and that the traveler will eventually be consumed by the sea, with his remains floating like flotsam:

> Il faut voir ces statues de liège sur les flots
>
> . . . .
>
> Quand l'esprit . . .
> Aperçoit l'avenir implacable sur les arêtes de la tombe
>
> It is necessary to see these statues of cork upon the waves
>
> . . . .
>
> When the mind . . .
> Perceives the implacable future upon the outlines of the tomb

However, to these terms of despair respond expressions of hope and solace: "Mais parfois la joie ouvre ses branches d'or au soleil/caressant/ L'amour épanoui ..." ("But sometimes joy opens its branches of gold in the/caressing sun/Love in full bloom ..." [369]). The exact result of this attempt at rebirth is never indicated, the ambiguity providing a chance for a positive interpretation amid Reverdy's pervasive gloom.

Refusing disorientation and psychological paralysis in "Reflux" ("Surging Back"), Reverdy associates poetic composition with the

motion of flowing, or more specifically, with the circulation of blood
as it journeys through the veins and receptacles of the body. Even
though the movement of flowing throughout Reverdy's work usually
refers to the theme of disorientation instead of orientation, it is occasionally found in a more positive context: "Un sang léger bouillonne à
grandes vagues dans des vases de prix. Il court dans les fleuves du corps,
donnant à la santé toutes les illusions de la victoire" ("A light blood
boils in great waves in precious vessels. It runs into the rivers of the
body, giving to health all the illusions of victory" [342–43]). Suggesting
the increased force of the blood as it passes through the receptacles,
the verb *bouillonner* refers to the amount of energy expended and its
transition into actual poetic creation. However, as sincere as the poet's
commitment is to creative movement, he fully realizes the illusory
nature of the voyage in the expression "toutes les illusions de la victoire." Recalling a traditional poetic formula, Reverdy imagines himself a voyager who, before dying, would like to free himself of his psychological burdens: "Ce soir je voudrais dépenser tout l'or de ma
mémoire, déposer mes bagages trop lourds" ("Tonight I would like to
consume all of the gold of my memory, set down my baggage too cum-
bersome" [343]). Perhaps the achievement of literary expression ("l'or
de ma mémoire") may remove the weight of death's threats, for
although the poet is finite, he in a sense realizes his own rebirth through
the poem.[2] Recalling the themes of descent and ascent of Rimbaud and
Mallarmé, Reverdy seeks the purest poetic inspiration in order that his
rebirth be complete:

Il faut remonter du plus bas de la mine, de la terre épaissie par l'humus du
malheur, reprendre l'air dans les recoins les plus obscurs de la poitrine, pous-
ser vers les hauteurs. . . .

It is necessary to reascend from the lowest point in the mine, from the earth
thickened by the humus of misfortune, to again take air into the most obscure
recesses of the chest, to push onward toward the heights. . . .

(343)

Expounding upon the descent into the mine, presented earlier in *Le
Gant de crin*, Reverdy interprets the journey not only as a means of
providing inspiration, but also of purifying semantic properties. By
slipping into the depths of the mind ("du plus bas de la mine," "les
recoins les plus obscurs"), past the layers of socially imposed verbal

connotations and customs ("l'humus du malheur"), the poet hopes to discover the basic meaning of words and expressions so that with a vocabulary untainted by society he may ascend intellectual heights, rising above the world of the quotidian into that of the purest realm of poetic inspiration.[3] It is through art that the transformation of the finite into the infinite may be realized.

A further explanation of the terms "toutes les illusions de la victoire" is found in "Lendemain de saison" ("Just After the Season") where the onrush of the waves overpower the poet and his literary inspiration: "Enfin le flot trop vigoureux qui me tourmente" ("Finally the wave too powerful which torments me"); "L'âme qui se dédore/Vers le sud la poussée tranquille de la mort" ("The soul which becomes tarnished/ Toward the south the tranquil thrust of death" [348]). The term *se dédorer* recalls the artistic decay suggested by *rouille* in the previous poem "Reflux." Unlike this latter text, the poet gives no mention of ascending the heights after having completed the descent into the subconscious: "Je descends plus bas dans la mine" ("I descend deeper into the mine" [349]). The mine, instead of a source of creativity, becomes the site for the poet's grave. It is the equivalent, then, of the abyss. With bitter disappointment the poet finds that a temporary stopover has become a permanent destination:

> Dans ma main seulement la cendre des tendresses
> Ou le sel de l'amour
> Le pain plus sec et le coeur trop rassis

> In my hand only the ashes of tenderness
> Or the salt of love
> The bread drier and the heart too stale

The chance for human infinity has been countered in this poem by the terms *sel, sec,* and *rassis,* all confirming the upheaval and disintegration alluded to in "Reflux" by such elements as rust, ashes, and dust. Elsewhere, in another poem, "La Coupe sombre" ("Somber Cutting"), the mine actually fills with mud, another element of decay: "Les roues de la fortune débrayées/Et la boue qui gonfle la mine" ("The wheels of fortune disconnected/And the mud which swells the mine" [367]). As the abyss is filled, the entire decaying structure of the poet's world collapses: "Les lourds paquets de désespoir s'écrasent" ("The heavy packages of despair collapse"); "Main aveugle main sans appel main inhabile" ("Blind hand hand without appeal inept hand"). Paradoxically, the abyss suggests a receptacle that has been filled but at the same time emptied.

The once-intriguing moments between arrival somewhere and reembarkation lose their mystery for the traveler. That the voyage has come to suggest irreversible passage downward into death is reflected in the title of the poem "Déroute" ("Downfall") where in a dream or vision living organisms watch their vital fluids trickling away:

> Et les gouttes de sang tiède dans les cheveux
> Dans les branches cassées où siffle la résine
> Et les doigts contre la poitrine arrêtée

> And the drops of tepid blood in the hair
> In the broken branches where the resin whistles
> And the fingers against the stilled breast
>
> (329)

The cooling temperature of the blood indicates that it no longer circulates. The resin, too, escapes from its natural cavity. As the liquids flow forth from the breach, the heart of both organisms, the person and the tree, lies exposed; the network of arteries now leads nowhere: "Le coeur disque signal ouvert des routes qui bifur/quent . . ." ("The heart a disc an open signal of roads which/fork" [329]).

Toward the end of *Ferraille* especially, Reverdy turns his often abrasive bitterness to the themes of self-deprivation and resignation before the specter time. Instead of the loss of blood or water, "Le Temps et moi" ("Time and Myself") describes the constant trickling forth of a glimmer of light, the terms "goutte à goutte" ("drop by drop" [376]) assuring a continuous recurrence of temporal sliding. A glass partition, perhaps in the sense of a mirror and hence a line of demarcation between past and present, or simply a barrier of protection, breaks, emphasizing the theme of rupture as in "Déroute": "La débâcle au bruit sec de la glace légère qui se brise/au réveil" ("The collapse with a dry noise of the light glass which breaks/at the moment of awakening" [376]). The glass is the final barrier between the poet and death. Its physical destruction not only indicates the end of all previous illusions but also the realities of his own mental breakdown.

The journey through the past, through dream, and finally into reality is repeated, and this time temporal passage appears as an undertow which erodes the outline of the coast, as well as that of the poet's body:

> Va-et-vient lumineux
> Ressac de la fatigue
> Goutte à goutte le temps creuse ta pierre nue
> Poitrine ravinée par l'acier des minutes
> Et la main dans le dos qui pousse à l'inconnu
>
> Luminous movement to and fro
> Undertow of fatigue
> Drop by drop time hollows out your bare stone
> Breast cut up by the steel of minutes
> And the hand in the back which pushes toward the unknown
>
> (377)

The terms "va-et-vient" and "ressac" suggest the regularity and relentless determination with which temporal destruction occurs. The erosion of the shoreline and also that of the poet's body find a parallel in the sculpture of the gravestone, as the poet's epitaph is chiseled out.

Now resigned to the ultimate destination, the poet makes no more attempts to reverse the direction of the journey downward into the abyss. Nightmares ensue in the poem "Coeur à la roue" ("Heart on the Wheel") which are filled with visions of the hole, abyss, or void, substitutes for the grave. The image of the blade reappears, severing all ties with the world of life:

> Je jetterai mon sort vide dans le fossé
>
> . . . .
> Je laisserai sur le tranchant du vide toutes les croix
> Tous les reflets perfides de l'espoir et de la chance
>
> I will cast my empty fate into the ditch
>
> . . . .
> I will leave behind upon the sharp edge of the void all the crosses
> All the treacherous reflections of hope and fortune
>
> (372)

The pit or abyss will not remain empty long, as Reverdy once more refers to the paradox of the void overflowing with particles of decay. During the course of his nightmare, he envisions his own body as it hardens into a stiff statue paralyzed like the memories in the poem "Tendresse": "Le bloc taillé dans la chair qui durcit/Cette statue intérieure que moi-même je sculpte" ("The block carved into flesh which hardens/This interior statue that I sculpture myself" [373]). The inner or interior statue of which the poet speaks may even be a death mask. This imagined death scene is reminiscent of that in the earlier poem "Il devait en effet faire bien froid" of *Pierres blanches;* however, the transference of movement from the tapestry folds to the corpse does not recur in the former poem where the statue is as motionless as the inscribed gravestone in "Le Temps et moi." The world of the living is now forever inaccessible to the poet; the statue has, in effect, been entombed: "Rien ne fera jouer les gonds rouillés de l'épaisse/portière" ("Nothing will force the rusted hinges of the thick/portal"). The flood waters of *Ferraille* have been stilled; the swollen arteries emptied. In settings dominated by immobility, there can be no hope for reconstruction. All that remains are traces—ashes, rust, mud, and scum—elements of erosion and dissolution.

CHAPTER 7

From Revolt to Resignation

A CURRENT of intense pessimism continues among Reverdy's last works, both in prose and poetry, where protest yields to resignation. As the flood waters of *Ferraille* recede, fragments of human lives lie motionless, disintegrating. Movement is often minimal in the collections *Plein verre* and *Bois vert*, yet at other times, for example, in *Le Chant des morts*, it is more intense and occurs in a destructive context not unlike the poems of *Ferraille*. Plagued by the frequent theme of the *épave*, the artist begins to view death with less horror, often accepting it as the final solution to a life of uncertainty where men are pawns manipulated by forces beyond their control. Yet, in his last prose work, *En vrac*, Reverdy emphasizes that there is one defense against the dissolution of the human spirit: through human creativity, art will record and preserve amid the abrupt rupture and dispersal that is human life.

I *Poetry*

A. Plein verre

The poet of *Plein verre* (*Full Glass*),[1] published in 1940, has lost his sense of protest; in this brief collection of poems, most of which continue the uniform margination of *Ferraille*, he is resigned to past failures and unresolved crises, and retains little hope for a future which is now beyond his control. The title itself, *Plein verre* or *Full Glass*, may refer to the poet's advancing years, and hence to a full or finished life or to the absence of youth and change. The full glass may also serve as a mirror as in *Flaques de verre*, reflecting an entire life, its past sorrows, and especially the incompleteness and inauthenticity which had always plagued Reverdy. In contrast to *Ferraille*, the themes of intense movement have all but disappeared, leaving only the shadow of a previous existence, which now prepares itself for death.

Poems such as "Arc-en-ciel" ("Rainbow") and "Crépuscule du matin" ("Dusk of the Morning") again recount ill-fated undertakings to reconstruct a portion of the poet's past. If in some texts such as "Une seule vague" ("Only One Wave"), Reverdy's spirit of revolt does return, it is only momentarily. Here, after choosing to live ("J'ai mis longtemps à me décider entre la vie et la/mort" ("I spent a long time deciding between life and/death" [387]), he resolves to fight the conflicting forces of fate ("Les contre-courants vertigineux de mon destin" "The vertiginous countercurrents of my destiny" [388]). The direction he chooses is forward into the fray:

> Il faut aller sur l'arête ensanglantée de la conquête
> Vers cette panoplie flambant à l'horizon
> . . . .
> Dans le tourbillon rouge des souvenirs
> Quand tout est refoulé par l'éclat de ce nouveau mystère
> . . . .
> Et de tout ce qui vit ailleurs
> Immobile et trop réel dans la matière
> Rien

> It is necessary to go upon the blood-stained ridge of conquest
> Toward this flaming armor on the horizon
> . . . .
> In the red whirlwind of memories
> When all is repressed by the flash of this new mystery
> . . . .
> And of all this which lives elsewhere
> Immobile and too real in matter
> Nothing

(388)

The terms "arête ensanglantée," "panoplie flambant," and "tourbillon rouge" are reminiscent of the red river ("Un ruisseau de sang clair" [381]) in the poem "Arc-en-ciel." The implication that the outcome of the conflict has been predetermined is suggested by the noun *conquête*. Movement and conflict cease, yielding to the state of void, so common in *La Lucarne ovale* and *Les Ardoises du toit*.

B.   Le Chant des morts

Written in a much more reserved tone of resignation, the collection *Le Chant des morts* (*Song of the Dead*)[2] relives Reverdy's pessimism and describes the aftermath of the destruction wrought in *Pierres blanches, Flaques de verre*, and *Ferraille*, especially voicing the bitterness and disillusions of this last work. Movement is more intense in this collection in which, as the title indicates, the victims are dominated by death and nightmare. Indeed, the poet's preference for a multitude of victims instead of a solitary sacrifice is a distinguishing feature of this work where there is a noticeable emphasis upon the suffering of "we" (*nous*) as opposed to only "I" (*je*). Although the *je* is by no means absent, Reverdy's frequent use of the *nous* suggests a sense of community, of belonging, of sharing, which is seldom found in his earlier poetry. Yet the tenor of *Le Chant des morts* is far from positive, for the multitude merely submits to the dissolution of the human spirit amid mud, ashes, and dust.

As an introduction to *Le Chant des morts*, the text "Il a la tête pleine d'or" ("He Has a Head Full of Gold"), one of the few poems of the collection composed in stanzas, describes the horror and agonies of death, first in the eyes of a solitary wayfarer and then in the nightmares of countless spectral figures. Reminiscent of Baudelaire's morose imagery and Nerval's spectral visions[3] is an image of a disfigured cadaver whose blood oozes forth, recalling also the stream of blood from the earlier text "Arc-en-ciel":

> La source de sang qui s'évente
> Quand la blessure au ventre
> Écoule son trésor aux franges du ruisseau
>
> The source of blood which rots
> When a stomach wound
> Empties its treasures into the banks of the river
> (401)

The cadaver is discovered during the course of a nightmare, for the poet speaks of a "nuit blanche" ("sleepless night"). It is very possible that, considering the period during which the collection was written—1944–1948—much of the torment and agony refers to World War II, Reverdy's own personal crises therefore partially coinciding and overlapping with those of a more universal nature. Indeed, the reference to a hospital would seem to support this interpretation ("La nuit glacée dans le sous-sol de l'hôpital"/"The frozen night in the basement of a hospital").

Besides the solitary voyager, the nightmare is peopled with numerous phantoms, ("Des êtres fabuleux"/"incredible beings") who then

find themselves accompanied by the communal *nous*. Successive elements of deterioration indicate that all will meet a similar fate: "les
moisissures d'un soleil" ("the mildews of a sun"); "le long fleuve des
jours noirs" ("the long river of black days"); "mousse desséchée"
("dried out moss" [402]). Perhaps again referring to a military context,
the poem describes the activities of the *nous*, now more aggressive and
more hopeful:

> Nous battons la campagne au coup
> Nous en avions la gorge pleine
> . . . .
> Il n'y a plus de place que pour l'espoir
> Dans le désert de la misère
>
> We are scouring the countryside to the beat
> We had our throats full of it
> . . . .
> There is no longer any room except for hope
> In the desert of misery
>
> (402)

Human suffering has become so great, the poet implies, as to preclude
greater sorrow; the only recourse lies in hope. The voyager knows now,
at least, that he is no longer alone: "Nous n'étions pas les seuls esclaves
à la chaîne" ("We were not the only ones enslaved"). However, the
courage that has been mustered is not sufficient for the ultimate confrontation. References to a final journey downward, which have
appeared earlier in other collections such as *Ferraille*, now again predominate and as in *Sources du vent*, human anguish is often associated
with the wind:

> Trop tard la peur casse les membres
> Le vent entasse nos soucis
> Trop tard il faut toujours descendre
> marche à marche dans l'infini
>
> Too late fear breaks the limbs
> The wind piles up our cares
> Too late it is still necessary to go down
> step by step into the infinite
>
> (402)

The confusion and disorientation in life are also present in death, described as "le labyrinthe des tombes" ("the labyrinth of tombs" [403]). Amid the mud, dirt, and decay, the poet speaks of a "cul-de-sac," the impasse or the absence of escape. As feared, the fetters of death close and permanently bind: "Les mains liées dans les ornières/ Les pieds au ciel" ("Hands bound to ruts/Feet to the sky").

The journey downward is associated with temporal passage in "Le Silence infernal" ("Infernal Silence") where, although it is narrated by the *je*, it is done so in view of memories provided by the suffering of *others*. The text is composed with a uniform left-hand margin which is characteristic of the collection as a whole. Dedicated to an anonymous group, "à tous ceux qui" ("to all those who"), the text brings together some of Reverdy's preferred themes and figures: accumulation appears in the form of welled-up temporal severities, the mirror is again a means of reflecting upon the storm which has left men shipwrecked, swirling eddies ("le remous") are reminiscent of the deadly whirlwind ("le tourbillon"), and finally, the lamp, like the mirror, serves as a vehicle of illumination upon past moments. Such themes and figures, though, are found in a context of death; efforts to illuminate or clarify the past only yield darkness and blood. Although the action of descent occurs amid the presence of *others*, there is no attempt to communicate. Forsaking the chance to comfort each other, extended hands remain empty: "On ne laisse entre les mains tendues aucune chance/Entre les coeurs reclus aucun mur mitoyen" ("One does not leave any chance between outstretched hands/Among recluse hearts no common wall" [450]). As the poem closes, Reverdy's frequent image of the *épave* reappears; during the descent the hearts have yielded to the extreme force of the wind, and are likened to ships without direction.

As the journey nears its end, the poet looks back upon his life with disappointment; between idea and reality lies only discrepancy. Along the side of a hill in "Longue portée" ("Long Range"), migratory birds wander, disoriented, and the poet can only wonder whether there are valid reasons for the tragedy in life: "Et tous ces hommes morts sans rime ni raison" ("And all these men dead without rhyme or reason" [433]). Admitting his disillusionment in the poem "Le Fil de feu" ("Thread of Fire"), Reverdy can only speak of the physical effects of deterioration; human vision has been blurred with false dreams which have collapsed: "Une boue d'illusions déborde le trottoir" ("A mud of illusions runs over the sidewalk" [414]). Whatever has not decayed or deteriorated has simply been effaced in "Le Poids des hommes" ("The Weight of Men") where nothing remains for the multitudes who again are compared to shipwreck victims:

> Il n'y a plus rien dans notre hémisphère
> Rien à boire
> Rien à dire
> Rien à voir
> . . . .
> Tant d'hommes perdus sur la route
> Tant de liens brisés entre le coeur et la tête
> Tant de navires en perdition
> . . . .
> Effacer étouffer l'image le souvenir
> le bruit
> Ne plus rien entendre
> Ni voir
>
> There is nothing anymore in our hemisphere
> Nothing to drink
> Nothing to say
> Nothing to see
> . . . .
> So many men lost along the route
> So many bonds broken between the heart and the head
> So many ships in distress
> . . . .
> To erase to stifle the image the memory
> the noise
> Not to hear anything any longer
> Nor see

> (417–18)

Repetition intensifies the poet's sense of futility. Hope spoken of in "Il a la tête pleine d'or" has been forever abandoned. Nor does the poet of "Le Sens du vide" ("Sense of the Void") try to cling to illusion: "Déliés dénoués rompus/Noeuds de l'espoir" ("Untied loosened broken/Knots of hope" [419]). The fears and predictions of previous collections have now been realized; the effects of upheaval and holocaust have been reenacted and then erased, and soon, the dead, those who have sung of the memories, will likewise still their voices, shaping and forming the neutral state.

C. Visages *and* Bois vert

There are two remaining collections of poetry from the postwar period: *Visages* (*Faces*) and *Bois vert* (*Green Wood*.) The former[4] is an anthology published in 1946 and drawn from poems of *Sources du vent* and *Plein verre*. The latter,[5] composed during the years 1946–1949, continues the tone of morose pessimism found in *Le Chant des morts*, yet reveals a slightly different emphasis. Narrated by the solitary voyager instead of the united *we* of Reverdy's last collection, it is written from the point of view of one who rejects life such as it has been given to him, severely twisted and restricted, as well as being in an advanced state of decay. Movement is only minimal; the theme of immobility found in Reverdy's early poetry predominates. Like green wood, unsuitable for warmth and comfort, man too, though of many years, does not fit into his environment. The horror of death has diminished, and it has finally come to represent a final resolution of torment despite its promise of nothingness. No longer willing to confront the illogic of the present, the artist looks ahead to the void where energies, at least, need no longer be wasted.

Reminiscent of the immobility and absence of color in "Les Blancs déserts de l'immortalité de l'âme" (*Flaques de verre*), the poem "Dans ce désert" ("In This Desert") describes a setting with no distinguishing features where all movement has been stilled and possible motion precluded. Connoted by the term *désert*, the sterility, lack of animation, dryness, and extreme restriction are reflected in the poet's repetition of negative expressions:

> Dans ce désert
>
> Enfin rien ne sort
> Rien ne vient
> . . . .
> Et décidément rien ne sort
> . . . .
> Rien ne répond à mon appel muet
> Rien ne s'oppose à ce geste durci
> qui fauche ma moisson
> . . . .
> Plus de feu dans le coin
> Plus d'amour plus de haine

> In this desert
>
> Finally nothing leaves
> Nothing comes
> . . . .
> And decidedly nothing leaves
> . . . .
> Nothing responds to my silent call
> Nothing opposes this harsh gesture
> which reaps my harvest
> . . . .
> No more fire in the corner
> No more love no more hatred
>   (528–29)

Retaining uniform margination as he does throughout the collection, Reverdy depicts a setting where seemingly nothing has happened, no psychological depression, no war, no torment. Nothing comes or goes, with future movement impossible as well: "Bateau perdu sans mât/ Sans orientation" ("Boat lost without a mast/Without orientation"). The poet/voyager is now forever stationary: "Fermé/Cercle de ma prison" ("Closed/Circle of my prison"). In a long enumeration, he sees himself devoid of the vital materials to continue life:

> Poitrine sans passion
>
> . . . .
> Amour sec
>
> . . . .
> mains vides
> sang perdu
>
> Dans ce désert
>
> Chest without passion
>
> . . . .
> Love dry
>
> . . . .
> hands empty
> blood lost
>
> In this desert
>   (529–30)

Accentuating the lack of motion are references to the theme of imprisonment, especially strong in the final poem of the collection, "Et maintenant" ("And Now"). Semantic flow bears no meaning whatsoever: "les mots n'ont plus de sens" ("words no longer have any sense" [532]). Beyond the point of escape, the human body begins to relax and become part of the process of neutralization. It is now delivered of all cares, having passed the last frontier and now reaching a comatose state. Death has come easily and painlessly, its setting is "le fond sombre du silence" ("the somber background of silence").

II *Prose: Closing Comments in* En vrac

Reverdy's resigned pessimism concludes in *En vrac* (*In Bulk*), a final collection of personal notes drawing together the disappointments of his last years following *Ferraille* as well as further comments upon the principal themes of his writing career. Written in an extremely personal tone, as with the earlier *Le Livre de mon bord, En vrac* shares with the reader the artist's reflections upon aesthetics, human nature, death, and religion. Published in 1956, the collection was most likely composed over a long period of time, for Reverdy speaks of having accumulated these notes during the course of thirty years.[6] These reflections seemingly occur with no chosen sequence or structure, but rather in the order of their conception, perhaps a reference to a further meaning of the terms *en vrac*, that is, having no specific packaging or preparation, in effect *pêle-mêle*. This connotation is indeed consistent with Reverdy's views of life and of the human struggle to seek a foothold.

Many of Reverdy's comments on aesthetics in *En vrac* restate what he had set forth earlier during the *Nord-Sud* era: the necessity of an autonomous work of art, the difference between the emotion inspiring the work of art and the emotion aroused by it, the simplicity of language, and the image theory.[7] In addition, as in *Le Gant de crin*, Reverdy reaffirms the interrelationship of everyday reality, deep reality, and the world of dream in the process of poetic transformation.[8] Regarding the degree of movement which shapes the initial germ of inspiration into the realized poem, Reverdy reconciles his desire for the constant, permanent elements in art, brought forth in *Le Gant de crin*, with his preference for continuous transformation, described in *Le Livre de mon bord*. Upholding his respect for equilibrium in art—"Un point commun entre la vie et l'art, c'est que, dans les deux, il s'agit de trouver l'équilibre dans l'instable" ("A common point between life and art is that in both it is a question of finding equilibrium in the unstable" [32])—Reverdy in *En vrac* sees the need to make the constant qualities in art adapt to the transformation that reality has become—"la vie est une perpétuelle désagrégation ..." (162). Poetry bearing thematic matter of universal scope and analyzing the torment and fragmentation, the utter destruction of the human soul, can survive and remain long after its creator has departed; it becomes a monument to the constant human desire to resist.[9]

Reverdy's view of human nature in *En vrac* is perhaps more pessimistic than in any of his earlier prose. Man as an individual is intelligent, sensitive, and kind; humanity in general, Reverdy finds, exhibits an animalistic nature: "imperfectible à l'infini" ("infinitely imperfectible" [7]). The dilemma of modern man, tossed haphazardly about into an unfriendly world, reappears as the poet's mood becomes one of his most pessimistic: "Apprendre à vivre, autant dire apprendre à mourir" ("Learning to live is as much as saying learning to die" [116]). By clinging to illusions such as happiness, a primitive human instinct, man only makes himself more miserable. Happiness cannot possibly be a goal, for each human being is condemned to death ("Comment pourrait-il avoir un *but* puisqu'il est un condamné à mort"/"How could he have a *goal* since he is condemned to death" [129]). Whatever false promises religions have made regarding human freedom (11–12), man is only the toy of an uncaring superior force (" ... il reste que nous n'en sommes pas du tout les maîtres mais seulement les plus dérisoires jouets"/" ... it remains that we are not at all the masters of it but only the most ridiculous toys" [125]). Reverdy's negative religious feelings voiced in *Le Livre de mon bord* become more explicit here, as he describes himself as "antireligious" (45). More definite also are Reverdy's ideas regarding suicide:

Comment, on ne vous a jamais demandé votre avis pour vous faire entrer dans ce monde, on vous interdirait—moralement d'en sortir comme vous voudriez et l'on appelle cette prison liberté! Ce n'était pas mal, et tout de même un plus supportable de s'être, du moins, donné un Dieu pour geôlier.

How, since one never asked your opinion to have you brought into this world, would one forbid you—morally to leave it as you would like and one calls this prison freedom! That was not too bad, and all the same a more tolerable situation to have given oneself, at least, a God as a jailer. (11)

And yet, as Reverdy has commented before in "Georges Braque, Une aventure méthodique," *La Liberté des mers, Grande nature, Ferraille,* and *Le Livre de mon bord,* human misery and suffering can be counterbalanced to some extent by rebirth through art. A work of art can rise above human baseness, endowing all that is finite with its own infinity: "Le but suprême de l'art, et depuis toujours oublié, aider l'homme à mieux supporter le réel—un apaisant reflet, moins aveuglant que le rayonnement direct du soleil" ("The supreme goal of art, and for a long time forgotten, to help man to better adapt to reality— an appeasing reflection, less blinding than the direct rays of the sun" [74]). Moreover, the act of writing is, for Reverdy, an opportunity to penetrate the wall of hostility which each man erects around himself.[10] Further developing this attitude in *En vrac,* Reverdy explains that poetry derives from what the poet lacks, in effect, from absence.[11] Its immortal, enduring qualities record the history of human longings, absence in effect is transformed into continuous presence:

> La poésie est dans ce qui n'est pas. Dans ce qui nous manque. Dans ce que nous voudrions qui fût. Elle est en nous à cause de ce que nous ne sommes pas. De ce que nous voudrions être. D'où nous voudrions être et où nous ne sommes pas.

> Poetry is in that which is not. In that which is lacking to us. In that which we would like to exist. It is in us because of that which we are not. Of that which we would like to be. Where we would like to be and where we are not.[12]

The absence which poetry signifies is positive, constituting what would restore order and happiness in human relationships. By virtue of its ephemeral germ, it cannot be easily accessible to all men, for such an availability would, indeed, expose it to human baseness. It remains for the poet, the untiring voyager, to narrate his absence, that is, to transform it from a vague *mystique* into realized, tangible presence.

CHAPTER 8

Conclusion

I T is somewhat ironic to note that in the work of a poet so dominated by rupture and extreme contradiction, there should be a unifying thematic center through which intersect imagery and poetic figures, supported by aspects of related form and style, and successions of closely associated themes. For Reverdy, the narration of countless journeys, the nucleus of his poetic thought, is the confession of a desperate need to reach out to *others*, countered by a tragic inability to do so. The journey may occur as a voyage through objective, tangible reality, an ascent into the ethereal, intellectual regions of the mind, or a descent into the repositories of the subconscious. Whatever the type of journey undertaken, the traveler encounters only hostile space, delineated either by a confusing overabundance of linear indications or by an acute dearth of orienting points. Lines of streets forming circular or spiral paths restrict movement and lead nowhere, the paralysis further reinforced by prepositions denoting a given shape such as *around*. When lines do intersect, in the present or past, it is a false union, for the crossroads can only signify indecision and irresolution.

Uncertainty at the crossroads becomes frustration and despair as the wayfarer's path is blocked with obstacles, usually images of closure— mirrors, doors, gates, bars, curtains, shutters, walls, houses—which occur in association with the room or chamber, places of artistic rebirth and human death respectively. In the latter case, given the absence of motion, obstacles accumulate, signifying a weighted, stagnant space. The selective spacing between the letters of words and entire semantic units within the text reinforces the atmosphere of isolated fragments as well as successive barriers. The frequent lack of transition seen in Reverdy's abrupt juxtaposition of images and the textual re-creation of superimposed objects as in his static poems of collage further limit movement. If the barrier is breached, it usually creates a false aperture, offering only a meaningless void. Desired objects and opportunity for communication with *others* are always just out of reach, "beyond," "behind," "beside," "at the edge of" the narrator, forever inaccessible. What is seemingly positive becomes negative, again with little transition, and an effect so often expressed by a statement of reversal in the last one or two lines of the text.

When the poet's interest turns away from the description of his expectations and from the activities of those who indifferently pass by, he exteriorizes through the themes of violent upheaval and disintegration his overwhelming fears and obsessions. The ever-threatening storm, the unsteadiness of objects observed, the effacement of entire settings and texts reveal a writer in great conflict with himself. Uncontrollable liquid outpourings reflected in angry seas, flood tides, rivers of blood and scum indicate the torrent of disillusion with which Reverdy's mind and spirit were beset. By selectively positioning lines of verse, he created the effects of multiplication and a confused thought sequence. Yet the intense dispersal caused by the whirlwind could be suddenly halted and transformed into a deserted setting, completely immobilized in decay, the device of reversal perhaps at its best.

If throughout his journeys Reverdy's efforts to participate in positive human communication were largely unsuccessful, as was his attempt to believe in a superior religious force, he did achieve a meaningful dialogue with his reader as he narrated the rupture and fragmentation of his soul. Whether or not he realized it at his death, his belief in art held true to his expectations; where spoken words had failed, the written expression breached the walls of contradictions, creating in effect a spiritual rebirth. The most accomplished poems, at least for this author, are to be found in *Les Ardoises du toit, Flaques de verre, Ferraille,* and *Le Chant des morts.* It is in these works that Reverdy became truly himself, finding his own individual means of expression rather than borrowing from sources around him. Reverdy's frustration with the problem of severely restricted space is perhaps best described in the first work, *Les Ardoises du toit,* whose title alone indicates the overlapping boundaries of the slates, rectangular lines which without transition encroach one upon the other. The states of tangible reality and dream or sleep begin and end just as abruptly, their thresholds and duration frequently traced by the varied spacing and margination of Reverdy's free verse. Although the new typography had first been tried in *Le Voleur de Talan,* it was accompanied in this earlier work with a heavier emphasis upon several current art movements. However, in

Les Ardoises du toit Reverdy's verse reveals greater assimilation of influences and a significant development of thematic material reinforced by typographical form. Mallarmé too had viewed the new typography as a structural element, but Reverdy experimented with it more extensively and used it with a greater variety of thematic material. Members of the young surrealist movement were exposed to Reverdy's aesthetics in *Nord-Sud* and *Self defence;* Aragon and Eluard incorporated varied spacing of terms and margination into their own poetry, and, of course, the group as a whole, especially Breton himself, was influenced by Reverdy's image theory. After Reverdy, the new typography would appear as a structural element in the work of a very modern poet, Marcelin Pleynet.

By the time *Flaques de verre* appeared, frustration had turned to bitter disappointment and violent protest. An uncaring God stood idly by while fragments of scum swept away all identifiable objects, all meaningful elements. Those who had been the victims of flood tides vainly searched for the places from which they had departed; settings were reduced to voids, slowly deteriorating in a state of advanced decay, interminably awaiting the return of their inhabitants. It is in *Ferraille* that the theme of deterioration is the most intense, where all elements are reduced to mud, ashes, scum, venom, and rust. Rupture is the most violent here where the poet makes countless references to dispersed human fragments, the *épaves* from shipwrecks. Whether overcrowded or deserted, space is meaningless in an atmosphere not unlike that created later by the existentialists. The new typography has been abandoned in Reverdy's later works of nightmare and horror; use of the traditional left-hand margin is quite uniform, the poet wishing to communicate his most desperate hours in the punctuated prose poem (*Flaques de verre*), the somber *verset* and more formal meters (*Ferraille*). The eerie stillness that comes just before the final threshold is crossed—from the door into the chamber, from the *lucarne* upward through the ceiling, from the lampshade back into the past, from the riverbank into the stream, from the frame of the picture into the personality of the subject, from the edge of the pool into its depth—is captured in *Le Chant des morts*. Resigned to the final voyage downward into the abyss, the poet has emptied his soul of the elements which have torn him apart, realizing that he too must now become part of the *absence* that constitutes the poetic germ. In these last three works especially, the reader is moved by the poet's sincerity and

extreme intensity of feeling, abhorring the brutal violence, yet knowing that he too must one day encounter it and live within its limitations.
However, the poet's creation will not have been lost, will not succumb
to the ashes of the abyss, but will faithfully reconstruct from the fragments the anxieties and obsessions that are contemporary *presence*.

Notes and References

Preface

1. Pierre Reverdy, *Le Livre de mon bord* (Paris, 1948), p. 94.
2. Charles Baudelaire, "Le Voyage" ("The Voyage"), in *Les Fleurs du mal* (Paris, 1964), p. 153.
3. "Igitur," in *Oeuvres complètes*, ed. Henri Mondor and G. Jean-Aubry (Paris, 1945), p. 443.
4. Mallarmé, *Oeuvres complètes*, pp. 32–33.
5. Arthur Rimbaud, "Lettre à Paul Demeny, 15 mai 1871," in *Poésies complètes* (Paris, 1963), p. 220. See also Anna Balakian's discussion of Rimbaud's descent into hell in *The Literary Origins of Surrealism* (New York, 1947), pp. 78–89.
6. *En vrac* (Monaco, 1956), p. 28.

Chapter One

1. Unless otherwise stated, all biographical data in this chapter can be found in Mortimer Guiney, *La Poésie de Pierre Reverdy* (Geneva, 1966).
2. Maurice Saillet, appendix, *Le Voleur de Talan*, by Pierre Reverdy (1917; reprint Paris, 1967), p. 168.
3. Robert W. Greene, *The Poetic Theory of Pierre Reverdy* (Berkeley, 1967), p. 9.
4. Greene, p. 12.
5. Grateful for Apollinaire's help, Reverdy wrote an article of gratitude in 1948 entitled "Le Coeur se souvient" ("The Heart Remembers"), which appeared in the November 18 issue of *Combat* and was later republished in Reverdy's *Cette émotion appelée poésie, écrits sur la poésie* (*This Emotion Called Poetry, Writings On Poetry*) (Paris, 1974), pp. 149–52.
6. For a detailed discussion of simultanism and futurism, see Pär Bergman's *Modernolatria et Simultaneità* (n.p., 1962).
7. Richard L. Admussen, "*Nord-Sud:* 1917–1918" (Ph.D. diss., University of Kansas, 1966), p. 26.
8. Greene, p. 14.
9. Bergman, p. 30, viii.
10. Guiney, p. 17.
11. Admussen, p. 26.
12. Ibid., p. 22.

13. Stanislas Fumet, appendix, *Le Gant de crin*, by Pierre Reverdy (1926; reprint Paris, 1968), p. 185.

14. Admussen, p. 32.

15. Ibid., p. 157.

16. Greene, p. 22.

17. Pierre Reverdy, "Fausses notes" ("False Notes"), *Verve* 7 (1952), 11: La grande inquiétude de l'homme ne lui vient pas de la mort. Ce sont les religions qui ont beaucoup contribué à la créer, à l'aggraver avec leurs promesses sinistres dans le bien et dans le mal, en tout cas la vie éternelle dans le feu ou dans le miel."

18. André Rousseaux quotes Pierre Reverdy in "La Poésie de Reverdy," *Le Figaro Littéraire*, December 10, 1949, p. 2: "Cette marche incertaine et précaire sur le vide. . . ."

19. Pierre Reverdy, "Lettre à Jean Rousselot, du 16 mai 1951," *Hommage à Pierre Reverdy—Entretiens sur les lettres et sur les arts*, ed. Luc Decaunes (n.p., n.d.), p. 16: " . . . la nature m'est apparue comme quelque chose d'hostile, d'inhumain, de terriblement angoissant, en lutte contre l'homme—; l'homme aux prises avec son rocher. . . ."

20. Pierre Reverdy, "Georges Braque Une aventure méthodique" ("Georges Braque A Systematic Adventure"), in *Note éternelle du présent, écrits sur l'art 1923–1960/Eternal Note of the Present, Writings On Art 1923–1960* (Paris, 1973), p. 54.

21. Ibid.

22. *Le Livre de mon bord*, pp. 190–91.

23. *En vrac*, p. 162: "Trait d'union du fini qui se désagrège perpétuellement (la vie est une perpétuelle désagrégation de la matière et même de l'esprit fini qui se transforment) avec l'infini sans déperdition."

Chapter Two

1. *Cale sèche*, in *Main-d'oeuvre* (Paris, 1949).

2. A sonnet by Mallarmé, "Le Vierge, le vivace et le bel aujourd'hui" ("The Virginal, Long-lived, and Beautiful Today"), describes a swan's attempts to escape, unsuccessful flights out of creative sterility. The literary effort is still-born in this poem from Mallarmé, *Oeuvres complètes*, p. 67:

Le vierge, le vivace et le bel aujourd'hui
Va-t-il nous déchirer avec un coup d'aile ivre
Ce lac dur oublié que hante sous le givre
Le transparent glacier des vols qui n'ont pas fui!

The virginal, long-lived, and beautiful today
Is it going to tear us with a drunken stroke of its wings
This hard, forgotten lake that under the frost is haunted by
The transparent glacier of flights which have not left!

3. Mallarmé, fearing that the banality of the everyday world ("les vieux jardins"; "the old gardens" from "Brise marine" ["Sea Breeze"] in Mallarmé, *Oeuvres complètes*, p. 38) and his own inner creative sterility ("Sur le vide papier que la blancheur défend"; "On the empty paper which whiteness defends") may jeopardize his poetic inspiration, feels compelled to depart upon a voyage into the beyond—"Fuir! là-bas fuir!" ("To flee! To flee there!")— into the realm of the Absolute.

Mallarmé views the voyage in a much more positive light than does Reverdy in "Tentative," for while it may fail, it represents his only chance to escape the intellectual boredom and uniformity of his present:—"Lève l'ancre pour une exotique nature!" ("Raise the anchor for an exotic nature!"). Reverdy, on the other hand, has almost convinced himself that his voyage/ literary attempt will fail, especially since *others* are intent upon the destruction of the flight.

4. The two lines "Il faut renouveler la façade des mots/De ceux qui veulent dire et qui ne peuvent pas" are especially reminiscent of Mallarmé in his "Le Tombeau d'Edgar Poe": "Donner un sens plus pur aux mots de la tribu" ("To give a purer sense to words of the tribe") in Mallarmé, *Oeuvres complètes*, p. 70.

5. For another analysis of the poem "Sujets," see Guiney, pp. 60–109.

6. The image of the fold, frequently found in Reverdy's early poems, generally connotes protection. This particular connotation may appear in only a physical sense as in the poem "Au carrefour des routes" from *Etoiles peintes* where Christ's plea descends among the folds of his garment, or, sometimes in a more intellectual sense, as in the poem "Bande de souvenirs."

Reverdy's preoccupation with the image of the fold is probably derived from his admiration for Mallarmé who greatly developed this theme, primarily in an intellectual context: folds provide a repository for past thoughts and deeds presently stagnant in the "Ouverture" ("Opening") of the "Hérodiade" (42), interior shelter for unexplored receptacles of literary genius in the prose work "Quant au livre" ("Regarding the Book" [370]), in Mallarmé, *Oeuvres complètes*.

7. In Reverdy's early poetry, the figure of the crossroads frequently connotes a moment of indecision for the poet who is caught between the legacies of the past and the avant-garde, or between his poetic craft and self-doubts, or even between the rut of everyday existence and the lure of a higher, intellectual sphere.

8. This decision is referred to in a general sense in the poems "Tentative" and "Sujets," but does not occur in a psychological context as in the poem "Bande de souvenirs."

9. The feathers represent a sacrificial image and suggest intellectual values abandoned subsequent to the resolution of emotional conflict. Mallarmé, from whom Reverdy has probably received inspiration here, links the image of the folds with that of the bird (*plis, plumes, ailes;* "wings"). The bird seeks to escape the sphere of mundane existence and tries to fly (*ailes*) toward the

azure, the sphere of artistic perfection, reflected within the folds of the ever-present fan (*éventail*). As the bird initiates flight, he often is hurt and sacrifices his feathers, just as the poet, who, struggling to write, sacrifices his own evergy and creative spirit. See Mallarmé's treatment of these images in the poems "Les Fenêtres," written in 1863 (32–33), and in "Le Démon de l'analogie" ("The Demon of Analogy"), written in 1864 (272–73), both in Mallarmé, *Oeuvres complètes*.

10. The point of resolution, a concept fundamental to surrealist doctrine, is treated by André Breton in his *Le Second manifeste (Second Manifesto)*, in Michel Carrouges, *André Breton et les données fondamentales du Surréalisme* (Paris, 1950), p. 23.

Tout porte à croire qu'il existe un certain point de l'esprit d'où la vie et la mort, le réel et l'imaginaire, le passé et le futur, le communicable et l'incommunicable, cessent d'être perçus contradictoirement. Or c'est en vain qu'on chercherait à l'activité surréaliste un autre mobile que l'espoir de détermination de ce point.

Everything leads us to believe that there exists a certain point within the mind from which life and death, the real and the imaginary, the past and the future, the communicable and the incommunicable, cease being perceived contradictorily. Now, it is in vain that one would seek to attribute to surrealist activity another motive than the hope of determining this point.

11. The poet Francis Ponge in the play *Le Savon (Soap)* (Paris, 1967) treats the theme of cleansing raw material received from inspiration. To a greater extent than Reverdy, Ponge develops the idea of water bubbling and foaming as a metaphor of transformation, from the poet's first intuitive feeling to the actual connotation born of the poetic word.

12. Throughout the poem "Voyage à Cythère" ("Voyage to Cytherea"), the poet witnesses his own demise as does the traveler in Reverdy's "Au saut du rêve." Baudelaire, however, is preoccupied with the physical devastation of the corpse: "De féroces oiseaux . . ./Détruisaient avec rage un pendu déjà mûr . . ." ("Savage birds . . ./Were voraciously destroying a man hung and already rotting . . ." [*Les Fleurs du mal*, p. 137]). Baudelaire seemingly experiences the humiliations of the corpse: "J'ai senti tous les becs et toutes les mâchoires" ("I felt all the beaks and all the jaws"). The poem, for Baudelaire, is purely allegorical, written with the intent of self-purgation and redemption: "Ah! Seigneur! donnez-moi la force et le courage/De contempler mon coeur et mon corps sans dégoût!" ("Oh! Lord! Give me the strength and the courage/To behold my heart and my body without disgust!" [138]).

Reverdy, who is not interested in physical disintegration here, emphasizes the solitude and the spatial context of death, its weight and thickness.

13. *Poèmes en prose* (Paris, 1915); reprinted in *Plupart du temps 1915–1922 (Most of the Time 1915–1922)*, (Paris, 1945), II, 29–55.

14. For example, Picasso's *La Famille de l'arlequin* (*The Harlequin's*

Family), private collection, New York, and *Famille de saltimbanques* (*Family of Tumblers*), National Gallery, Washington, D.C., both cited in Maurice Sérullaz, *Le Cubisme* (Paris, 1963), p. 61. Reverdy greatly admired Picasso and wrote the text *Pablo Picasso et son oeuvre* (*Pablo Picasso and His Work*), (Paris, 1924), although it was probably written several years earlier. It has been republished in *Nord-Sud, Self defence, et autres écrits sur l'art et la poésie 1917–1926* (*Nord-Sud, Self defence, and Other Writings on Art and Poetry 1917–1926*), (Paris, 1975).

15. *Femme à la guitare*, collection of M. Raoul La Roche, Paris; John Golding, *Le Cubisme*, trans. Françoise Cachin (Paris, 1962); illus. 39.

16. For more cubist theory, see Gerald Kamber's *Max Jacob and the Poetics of Cubism* (Baltimore, 1971), p. 22.

17. *Quelques poèmes* (Paris, 1916); reprinted in *Plupart du temps 1915–1922*, I, 59–72.

18. Another cubist technique, and in effect, a type of collage, is the *papier collé* (pasted paper literally), with the basic difference being that the pasted objects are made of paper, and principally grouped for pattern than for symbolism, Golding, pp. 94–97. Reverdy wrote an introduction to a collection of lithographs by Henri Laurens (*Henri Laurens: papiers collés*, Paris, 1955) in praise of the freedom which this technique provided.

19. Sérullaz, pp. 110–11.

20. Golding. p. 151.

21. *Nu descendant l'escalier*, Philadelphia Museum of Art, Philadelphia; Golding, illus. 70b.

22. Golding, p. 151.

23. For more discussion on the theme of the voyage as treated by Baudelaire, Mallarmé, Rimbaud, and Reverdy, see the preface and pp. 136, 159, 164–65.

24. "Traits et Figures" ("Lines and Shapes"), in *Poèmes en prose*, p. 35; italics mine.

25. This poem supposedly received its inspiration from time spent at the Bibliothèque Nationale. Guiney (p. 119) quotes a remark Reverdy made, later recalled by Blaise Cendrars, which pinpoints the setting.

26. Jean-Pierre Richard in his *Onze études sur la poésie moderne* (Paris, 1964) defines the Reverdian wall as "Le mur, c'est bien l'être lui-même, mais l'être refusé, retourné, et devenu non-être" ("The wall is existence itself, but existence refused, overturned, and having become nonexistence" [15]). The line which forms the wall, he sees as "the enemy" because "elle enserre une réalité qui se voudrait illimitée" (". . . it encompasses a reality which wishes to be boundless" [27]).

27. Jean Schroeder, "The Theme of Movement in the Poetry of Pierre Reverdy" (Ph.D. diss., City University of New York, 1975).

28. *La Lucarne ovale* (Paris, 1916); reprinted in *Plupart du temps 1915–1922*, I, 75–159.

29. Anthony Rizzuto, *Style and Theme in Reverdy's Les Ardoises du toit* (University, Ala., 1971).

30. *La Liberté des mers* (Paris, 1960).

Chapter Three

1. Admussen, pp. 34, 37, 39.

2. *Les Peintres cubistes* (Paris, 1913), p. 13, quoted in Admussen, p. 142.

3. "Nord-Sud," in *Nord-Sud, Self defence, et autres écrits sur l'art et la poésie 1917–1926*, p. 20.

4. Admussen, p. 65.

5. "Nord-Sud," in *Nord-Sud, Self defence, et autres écrits sur l'art et la poésie 1917–1926*, p. 45.

6. Everett Franklin Jacobus, Jr., "Pierre Reverdy and the Poetry of Cubism: Literary Responses to a Revolution in Art" (Ph.D. diss., Cornell University, 1971), p. 219.

7. "Nord-Sud," in *Nord-Sud, Self defence, et autres écrits sur l'art et la poésie 1917–1926*, p. 95.

8. Although he sought to avoid the label of cubist poet, Reverdy continued to defend the movement and used the literary journal *Sic* as an additional means of support for cubist theory. Welcomed by Pierre Albert-Birot, an article by Reverdy in defense of the cubists, "Vociférations dans la clarté" ("Outcries in Clarity"), was published in the October, 1918 issue. It later reappeared in *Nord-Sud, Self defence, et autres écrits sur l'art et la poésie 1917–1926*, pp. 127–30; For further discussion, see the notes of this work, pp. 308–10.

9. Admussen, p. 139.

10. "Nord-Sud," in *Nord-Sud, Self defence, et autres écrits sur l'art et la poésie 1917–1926*, pp. 33–34.

11. Admussen, pp. 59–61.

12. Jacobus, p. 238.

13. "Nord-Sud," in *Nord-Sud, Self defence, et autres écrits sur l'art et la poésie 1917–1926*, p. 73.

14. Jacobus, p. 234.

15. Etienne-Alain Hubert, notes, *Nord-Sud, Self defence, et autres écrits sur l'art et la poésie 1917–1926*, p. 283.

16. Admussen, p. 143.

17. Jacobus, p. 274.

18. Ibid., p. 336.

19. "Nord-Sud," in *Nord-Sud, Self defence, et autres écrits sur l'art et la poésie 1917–1926*, p. 62.

20. Admussen, p. 139.

21. Hubert, notes, in *Nord-Sud, Self defence, et autres écrits sur l'art et la poésie 1917–1926*, p. 286.

22. Admussen, pp. 100–101.

23. *Self defence* (Paris, 1919); reprinted in *Nord-Sud, Self defence, et autres écrits sur l'art et la poésie 1917–1926*, pp. 103–24.

24. See notes concerning Mallarmé and Ponge, pp. 159–60, 166.

25. Greene, p. 43.

26. *Self defence*, p. 119.

27. Greene, p. 17.

28. Saillet, appendix, in *Le Voleur de Talan*, p. 158.

29. Such a colorless palette is characteristic of cubist paintings, especially those of Braque and Picasso during the analytical period.

30. The poet re-creates here his lonely arrival in Paris described at the beginning of *Le Voleur de Talan*, yet the reader will remember repetitions of similar scenes in the past—the disappointingly circular itinerary, the return to the point from which one began ("Voyages trop grands," in *Poèmes en prose*, p. 48), the paradoxical isolation experienced within a multitude of people, the irreality of memories and events which cannot be shared ("Une apparence médiocre," in ibid., pp. 39–40; "D'un autre ciel," in *La Lucarne ovale*, pp. 110–11).

31. *Au Soleil du plafond* (Paris, 1955). Some of the poems contained in this work come from two manuscripts referred to in the notes by Hubert in *Nord-Sud, Self defence, et autres écrits sur l'art et la poésie 1917–1926*, p. 343: *Le Cadran quadrillé* (*The Squared Dial*) and *Entre les 4 murs et sur la table* (*Between the Four Walls and On the Table*), the first written about 1916, the second perhaps a little earlier.

32. *Les Jockeys camouflés* (Paris, 1918); reprinted in *Plupart du temps 1915–1922*, II, 9–24.

33. *Les Ardoises du toit* (Paris, 1918); reprinted in *Plupart du temps 1915–1922*, I, 163–245.

34. "Les Jockeys camouflés," in *Plupart du temps 1915–1922*, II, 21.

35. Apollinaire in his collection *Calligrammes* (1918; reprint Paris, 1925) pursued a pictorial objective in his free arrangement of verse, seeking in effect to sketch the object(s) in question—"Paysage" ("Countryside"), "Lettre-Océan" ("Ocean-gram"), "La Cravate et la montre" ("The Tie and the Watch"), pp. 27, 43, and 53 respectively. However, neither Mallarmé, who had used typography as a structural element in the text "Un coup de dés/A Throw of the Dice" (1897) (in Mallarmé, *Oeuvres complètes*, pp. 455–77), nor Reverdy sought a graphic representation.

36. As early as *Poèmes en prose* Reverdy reveals his obsession with restricting partitions: "Dans ma tête des lignes, rien que des lignes" ("Traits et figures" [35]) and "De mes ongles j'ai griffé la paroi . . ." ("L'Esprit sort"

[43]). Limited movement in *Les Ardoises du toit* is indicated in the arrangement of slates whose surfaces partially overlap, emphasizing a superimposed network of lines re-created artistically in the substantives *seuil, paupière, rideau, rive, volet,* etc.

37. *La Guitare endormie* (Paris, 1919); reprinted in *Plupart du temps 1915-1922,* II, 27-63.

38. "Sujets" discussed on pp. 25-28.

39. One of the best examples of this anonymity comes from the text "Le Nouveau venu des visages" ("The Newcomer Among the Faces") of *La Guitare endormie: "Toutes les têtes se retournent pour deviner le nom/approximatif de ce nouveau visage"* ("All heads turn to guess the approximate/name of this new face" [53]).

Chapter Four

1. *Etoiles peintes* (Paris, 1921); reprinted in *Plupart du temps 1915-1922,* II, 67-86.

2. *Coeur de chêne* (Paris, 1921); reprinted in *Plupart du temps 1915-1922,* II, 89-107.

3. *Cravates de chanvre* (Paris, 1922); reprinted in *Plupart du temps 1915-1922,* II, 111-43.

4. *Epaves du ciel* (Paris, 1924), includes *Poèmes en prose, Quelques poèmes, La Lucarne ovale, Les Ardoises du toit, Les Jockeys camouflés, La Guitare endormie, Etoiles peintes, Coeur de chêne,* and *Cravates de chanvre.*

5. *Ecumes de la mer* (Paris, 1925).

6. Grande nature (Paris, 1925); reprinted in *Main-d'oeuvre,* pp. 9-37.

7. "Le Dormeur du val," in Rimbaud, *Poésies complètes,* p. 40.

8. *La Balle au bond* (Marseille, 1928); reprinted in *Main-d'oeuvre,* pp. 41-77.

9. *Risques et périls* (1930; reprint Paris, 1972).

10. *La Peau de l'homme* (1926; reprint Paris, 1968).

11. Shortly after "La Peau de l'homme," Reverdy published another text in honor of Picasso's work, "Pablo Picasso" which appeared in the review *Paris-Journal* on December 14, 1923. It discussed Picasso's objectives as a cubist as well as his place in art beyond the limits of cubism. Then, in 1952, Reverdy published "Un Oeil de lumière et de nuit" ("An Eye of Light and of Night") in the October issue of *Le Point,* followed by "Solidarity of the Genius and the Dwarf" which first appeared in *Art News Annual* in 1957. These articles can all be found in *Note éternelle du présent, écrits sur l'art, 1923-1960* and appear on pages 191-204, 207-17, and 233-43 respectively.

12. Reverdy's descent into the world of dreams recalls Rimbaud's plunge into hell. For Reverdy, the voyage downward is much less violent. Like Rim-

baud he seeks to free the imagination of the bonds imposed by logic, and thereby to enrich the sources of poetic inspiration. However, Reverdy is more concerned with exposing the creative soul to as many planes of reality as possible than with letting it come to know itself through the destructive forces of chaos and immoderation. Rimbaud's voyage into hell is an exploration by the soul of the depths of its subconscious. The plunge into the world of dreams, as interpreted by Reverdy, is "an increase in awareness through the total liberation of the imagination," the dream itself signifying "a kind of rêverie poétique" (Greene, p. 49). See also Anna Balakian's discussion of Rimbaud's descent into hell in *The Literary Origins of Surrealism* (New York, 1947), pp. 78–79.

13. *Le Gant de crin*, p. 17. This description of the dream also appeared in the article "Le Rêveur parmi les murailles."

14. This reference to the crossroads of dream and reality first appeared in "Le Rêveur parmi les murailles."

15. "Deep reality" and the sovereignty of the senses are incompatible and therefore, the real ("le réel") cannot exist in the realm of material objectivity. Naturalism is, according to Reverdy, an example of complete submission to sensory perceptions.

16. These references to the poet's descent were made in an article in *Le Journal littéraire* of June 7, 1924, entitled "Poésie" and in "Le Rêveur parmi les murailles." The first article has also been reprinted in *Nord-Sud, Self defence, et autres écrits sur l'art et la poésie 1917–1926*.

17. This preference for static art may also be interpreted as a negative comment on futurism. Later in "Note éternelle du présent" ("Eternal Note of the Present") which appeared in the *Minotaure* of June 1, 1933, Reverdy continued to extoll the static quality of art. Yet at the same time he maintained that static art and dynamic art were not opposites, but instead that the latter was a type of art in which the former was respected and utilized. This article was reprinted in *Note éternelle du présent, écrits sur l'art, (1923–1960)*, pp. 19–20.

18. Carrouges, p. 135.

19. André Breton, *Manifestes du surréalisme* (Paris, 1924), p. 51.

20. Greene, p. 52.

21. Gabriel Bounoure, "Pierre Reverdy et sa crise religieuse de *1925–1927*," in *Pierre Reverdy 1889–1960* (Paris, 1962), p. 199.

22. Anna Balakian, "The Surrealist Image," *The Romanic Review*, December, 1953, p. 274. See also Carrouges, pp. 142, 165.

23. *Le Gant de crin*, p. 120.

24. Greene, p. 52.

25. *Le Gant de crin*, p. 74.

26. Ibid., p. 74; Baudelaire, "Mon coeur mis à nu" ("My Heart Laid Bare").

Chapter Five

1. *Sources du vent* (Paris, 1929); reprinted in *Main-d'oeuvre*, pp. 81–252.

2. The indifference of nature is especially apparent in the poems "Souffle d'ouest" ("Breeze From the West"), "Fausse joie" ("False Joy"), "L'Eau dort" ("Water Sleeps"), "Bruits du soir" ("Noises of Evening"), and "N'Essayez pas" ("Don't Try"), all in *Grande nature*, pp. 11–12, 20–21, 22–23, 26–27, 24–25.

3. *Pierres blanches* (Carcassonne, 1930); reprinted in *Main-d'oeuvre*, pp. 255–323.

4. *Flaques de verre* (1929; reprint Paris, 1972).

5. *Le Livre de mon bord*, p. 7.

Chapter Six

1. *Ferraille* (Brussels, 1937); reprinted in *Main-d'oeuvre*, pp. 327–77.

2. The realization of human infinitude through art is a theme already discussed in *La Liberté des mers, Grande nature* ("Détresse du sort"), and "Georges Braque Une Aventure méthodique." It will be treated again in *En vrac.*

3. As early as *Self defence* Reverdy's contention that "Un élément ne devient *pur* que dégagé du sentiment que lui confère sa situation dans la vie. Il faut le dépouiller de ce sentiment . . ." ("An element only becomes *pure* when separated from the feeling which its context/setting in life gives to it. It is necessary to divest it of this feeling . . ." [120])˙ is reminiscent of Mallarmé's "donner un sens plus pur aux mots de la tribu" (Mallarmé, *Oeuvres complètes*, p. 70). (Italics are mine.)

The desire to arrive at the basic meaning of words and expressions will be further studied by Ponge who will discover a parallelism between the physical and verbal worlds. According to this poet, various meanings of words derive from connotations which are arbitrary, utilitarian, and banal, imposed by a society which has betrayed the natural and primitive properties of the words themselves. Therefore, any attempt at communication, either oral or written, can only fail. Ponge's solution to this dilemma would be the disfigurement of language, removing every arbitrary and utilitarian meaning. By restoring true semantic density to the word, the physical density of the referent would also be realized at the same time. From this type of oral exercise there would result semantic creation, true meaning. For Ponge, perhaps the most important result is the very act of *creating*, of *becoming* which he terms "l'acte de verbalisation" (Jean-Paul Sartre, *L'Homme et les choses* [Paris, 1947], unpaged). See also Philippe Sollers, *Entretiens de Francis Ponge avec Philippe Sollers* (Paris, 1970).

Chapter Seven

1. *Plein verre* (Nice, 1940); reprinted in *Main-d'oeuvre*, pp. 381–97.
2. *Le Chant des morts* (Paris, 1948); reprinted in *Main-d'oeuvre*, pp. 401–52.
3. See Baudelaire's "L'Irréparable" ("The Irretrievable"), pp. 67–69; "La Cloche fêlée" ("The Cracked Bell"), p. 85; "Danse macabre" ("Dance of Death"), pp. 113–15, all in *Les Fleurs du mal*. See Gérard de Nerval's *Aurélia* (1855; reprint Paris, 1964), especially pp. 78, 83.
4. *Visages* (Paris, 1946).
5. "Bois vert," in *Main-d'oeuvre*, pp. 517–33.
6. *En vrac*, p. 147.
7. Greene, p. 88.
8. *En vrac*, pp. 4–5.
9. Reverdy in *En vrac* sees human life set in a cycle of happiness/unhappiness. Man would become bored if he were completely satisfied and fulfilled: "Il lui faut être troublé et rassuré alternativement, être ému et le plus fortement, puis calmé, apaisé, afin de reprendre sa force, retrouver l'équilibre et la sérénité d'un moment. Et puis recommencer" ("It is necessary for him to be alternately troubled and reassured, to be moved and in the strongest way, then calmed, appeased, in order to collect his strength, to again recover the equilibrium and serenity of a moment. And then to begin again" [20]).
10. Reverdy states in *Le Livre de mon bord*, p. 234: "On écrit pour sortir de soi, pour se sentir un peu plus fermement un autre en face de soi" ("One writes to escape oneself, to experience a little more concretely *another* opposite oneself," italics mine).
11. This idea also appears in "Circonstances de la poésie" ("Circumstances of Poetry"), *L'Arche*, no. 21 (1946), 3–9. The article was reprinted in *Cette émotion appelée poésie, écrits sur la poésie*, pp. 41–42.
12. *En vrac*, p. 139.

Selected Bibliography

PRIMARY SOURCES

Poèmes en prose. Paris: Imprimerie de Birault, 1915.
Quelques poèmes. Paris: Imprimerie de Birault, 1916.
La Lucarne ovale. Paris: Imprimerie de Birault, 1916.
Nord-Sud, no. 1 (March, 1917). Articles published under Reverdy's direction and editing. The last issue, no. 16, appeared in October, 1918.
Le Voleur de Talan. 1917; reprint Paris: Flammarion, 1967.
Les Jockeys camouflés. Paris: A la Belle Edition, 1918.
Les Ardoises du toit. Paris: Imprimerie de Birault, 1918.
Self defence. Paris: Imprimerie Littéraire, 1919.
La Guitare endormie. Paris: Editions Nord-Sud, 1919.
Etoiles peintes. Paris: Editions Kra, 1921.
Coeur de chêne. Paris: Galerie Simon, 1921.
Cravates de chanvre. Paris: Editions Nord-Sud, 1922.
Epaves du ciel. Paris: NRF, 1924. Includes *Poèmes en prose, Quelques poèmes, La Lucarne ovale, Les Ardoises du toit, Les Jockeys camouflés, La Guitare endormie, Etoiles peintes, Coeur de chêne*, and *Cravates de chanvre*.
Ecumes de la mer. Paris: NRF, 1925. Includes selections from *La Lucarne ovale, Les Ardoises du toit*, and *La Guitare endormie*.
Grande nature. Paris: Editions des Cahiers Libres, 1925.
Le Gant de crin. 1926; reprint Paris: Flammarion, 1968.
La Peau de l'homme. 1926; reprint Paris: Flammarion, 1968.
La Balle au bond. Marseilles, Editions des Cahiers du Sud, 1928.
Sources du vent. Geneva: Editions des Trois Collines, 1929.
Flaques de verre. 1929; reprint Paris: Flammarion, 1972.
Risques et péril. 1930; reprint Paris: Flammarion, 1972.
Pierres blanches. Carcassonne: Editions Jordy, 1930.
Ferraille. Brussels: Cahiers du Journal des Poètes, 1937.
Plein verre. Nice: Editions des Iles de Lérins, 1940.
Plupart du temps 1915–1922, I and II. Paris: Gallimard, 1945. Includes *Poèmes en prose, Quelques poèmes, La Lucarne ovale, Les Ardoises du toit, Les Jockeys camouflés, La Guitare endormie, Etoiles peintes, Coeur de chêne*, and *Cravates de chanvre*.
Visages. Paris: Editions du Chêne, 1946. Includes selections from *Sources du vent* and *Plein verre*.

Le Chant des morts. Paris: Tériade, 1948.

Le Livre de mon bord. Paris: Mercure de France, 1948.

Main-d'oeuvre. Paris: Mercure de France, 1949. Includes *Cale sèche, Grande nature, La Balle au bond, Sources du vent, Pierres blanches, Ferraille, Plein verre, Le Chant des morts*, and *Bois vert*.

"Fausses notes." *Verve* 7 nos. 27–28 (1952), 9–15.

Au Soleil du plafond. Paris: Tériade, 1955.

Henri Laurens: papiers collés. Paris: Berggruen, 1955.

En vrac. Monaco, Editions du Rocher, 1956.

La Liberté des mers. Paris: Maeght, 1960.

Note éternelle du présent, écrits sur l'art 1923–1960. Paris: Flammarion, 1973.

Cette émotion appelée poésie, écrits sur la poésie. Paris: Flammarion, 1974.

Nord-Sud, Self défence, et autres écrits sur l'art et la poésie 1917–1926. Paris: Flammarion, 1975.

SECONDARY SOURCES

1. Studies of Reverdy

ADMUSSEN, RICHARD L. "*Nord-Sud:* 1917–1918." Ph.D. dissertation, University of Kansas, 1966. Informative, thorough study of Reverdy's journal outlining the literary climate of his early years in Paris; interesting section on futurist and simultanist aesthetics; discussion of collaborators, goals, and aesthetics of the journal as well as later influence.

BACHAT, CHARLES. "Reverdy et le surréalisme." *Europe*, no. 475–476 (November–December, 1968), 79–100. Reverdy's imagery and its influence upon Breton.

DECAUNES, LUC, ed. *Hommage à Pierre Reverdy—Entretiens sur les lettres et sur les arts*. Paris: Subervie Editeur/Rodey, n.d. An interesting collection of letters and articles of which some of the best are: several personal letters written by Reverdy about his early life and the hostility of nature together with extracts of some of his articles on aesthetics; a discussion by Gabriel Bounoure, "Notes marginales sur Pierre Reverdy," treating the negativism with which Reverdy's poetry creates "anti-poems"; Jean-Charles Gaudy's "Les Chemins solitaires" which outlines the differences between Breton's view of the image and Reverdy's; an analysis by Renée Riese-Hubert, "L'Elan vers l'humain—*La Lucarne ovale* et *Le Chant des morts*," of the restrictive element in Reverdy's poetry, especially with respect to some prepositions and adverbs, and in addition, a comparison between rampant destruction in *La Lucarne ovale* and completed ruin in *Le Chant des morts*.

DU BOUCHET, ANDRÉ. "Envergure de Reverdy." *Critique*, April, 1951, pp. 308–20. Contrast and sudden change in Reverdy's poetry.

FUMET, STANISLAS. Appendix. In *Le Gant de crin*, by Pierre Reverdy. Paris:

Flammarion, 1968. Invaluable correspondence relating to the publication of *Le Gant de crin* with interesting background details of Reverdy's attitude at the time.

GEAY, JEAN-PIERRE. "La Quête du Réel dans l'oeuvre poétique de Pierre Reverdy." *Revue d'esthétique,* no. 2 (1970), 189–203. Instability of Reverdy's settings.

GREENE, ROBERT W. *The Poetic Theory of Pierre Reverdy.* University of California Publications in Modern Philology, vol. 82. Berkeley: University of California Press, 1967. Brilliant, thorough work beginning with Reverdy's early years in Paris, his friendships with Apollinaire and Jacob, the aesthetics of cubism, futurism, and simultanism and their influence upon Reverdy; *Nord-Sud, Self defence,* and the development of Reverdy's theories of aesthetics, particularly his interpretations of the image, dream, thought; Reverdy and his rapports with Valéry, surrealism, Baudelaire, and Malraux.

————. "Pierre Reverdy, Poet of Nausea." *PMLA* 85 (January, 1977), 48–55. Excellent analysis of instability of setting and images of collapse in Reverdy's poetry; Reverdy's affinity with existententialist mode of thinking.

GUINEY, MORTIMER. *La Poésie de Pierre Reverdy.* Geneva: Librairie de l'Université, Georg & Cie., 1966. Thorough study of Reverdy's relations with the Parisian art milieu and a sensitive and creative analysis of his poetry with selections examined by *explications de texte;* relationships among fundamental themes as they recur from text to text; comparisons of Reverdy with Baudelaire, Rimbaud, Mallarmé, Valéry, and Sartre; emphasis on poetry and aesthetics rather than prose works; bibliography one of the best.

————. "Cubisme, Littéraire et Plastique." *Revue des Sciences Humaines,* no. 142 (April–June, 1971), 271–81. Rapports between Reverdy and the cubist image.

HUBERT, ETIENNE-ALAIN. Notes. In *Nord-Sud, Self defence, et autres écrits sur l'art et la poésie 1917–1926,* by Pierre Reverdy. Paris: Flammarion, 1975. Well-organized, highly informative presentation of relevant details about articles which had previously been obscure and unknown.

HUSSON, JULIA. "Pierre Reverdy and the Poème-objet." *Australian Journal of French Studies* 5, no. 1 (January–April, 1968), 21–34. The cubist phase of Reverdy's poetry; brief stylistic analysis.

JACOB, SARAH FRANCES. "The Man and the Poet in the Work of Pierre Reverdy." Ph.D. dissertation, Tulane University, 1956. Summary of Reverdy's life as reflected in works, particularly in *Le Voleur de Talan;* surrealists' reaction to Reverdy's imagery; discussion of depth images and the theme of the voyage.

JACOBUS, EVERETT FRANKLIN, Jr. "Pierre Reverdy and the Poetry of Cubism: Literary Responses to a Revolution in Art." Ph.D. dissertation, Cornell

University, 1971. Excellent study of the aesthetics of the *Nord-Sud* journal with discussion of cubist theory, Reverdy's cubist poetry, and the work of Apollinaire, Cendrars, and Jacob as related to *Nord-Sud* and cubism. Excellent bibliography.

Pierre Reverdy 1889–1960. Paris: Mercure de France, 1962. The best collection of comments on Reverdy and his work. Among the most interesting are: Blaise Cendrars and the origin of "L'Esprit sort" in "Sortant de la Nationale;" a discussion of the cubist elements in Reverdy's poetry by Stanislas Fumet in "La Poésie plastique de Pierre Reverdy"; the ephemeral quality of Reverdy's art and the state of *attente* as analyzed in Mario Maurin's "Le Moment de passage"; extracts from some of Reverdy's letters accompanied by comments of Emma Stojkovic-Mazzariol, "En marge d'une correspondance," an article emphasizing Reverdy's obsession with universal collapse and his belief in the value of poetry; a comparison of Reverdy's imagery with that of the surrealists by Gabriel Bounoure, "Pierre Reverdy et sa crise religieuse de 1925–1927"; Georges Poulet's commentary on Reverdy and the figure of the wall, "Reverdy et le mystère des murs"; discussion of passage and slipping in "Le Gré du vent" by Pierre Schneider; Reverdy's treatment of space together with the figure of the wall and instability of setting in "Reverdy Entre Deux Mondes" by Jean-Pierre Richard.

RICHARD, JEAN-PIERRE. *Onze études sur la poésie moderne*. Paris: Editions du Seuil, 1964. Brilliant analysis of relationships among fundamental themes of space such as thickness and distance, the void, wall, and line with comments on the motion of spinning and slipping.

RIZZUTO, ANTHONY. *Style and Theme in Reverdy's Les Ardoises du toit*. University, Ala.: University of Alabama Press, 1971. Informative discussion of Reverdy's background, era, and Reverdy scholars. Thorough stylistic analysis and excellent comments on poetic technique, especially the chapters on vocabulary, word order, and "visual verse."

———. "Metaphor in Pierre Reverdy's *Ferraille*." *Kentucky Romance Quarterly* 22 (1975), 321–34. Interesting view of the themes of creation and destruction in *Ferraille* seen through the contradictions within the artist, his aesthetic and religious "uncertainties."

ROUSSEAUX, ANDRÉ. "La Poésie de Reverdy." *Le Figaro Littéraire*, December 10, 1949, p. 2. Insecurity of human existence.

———. "Sagesse de Reverdy." *Le Figaro Littéraire*, June 2, 1956, p. 2. Reverdy's pessimism regarding human character and intense religious doubt.

ROUSSELOT, JEAN, and MANOLL, MICHEL. *Pierre Reverdy*. Poètes d'aujourd'hui. Paris: Editions Seghers, 1951. Good introduction to Reverdy's work, good descriptions of the atmosphere in his settings; little thematic and stylistic analysis; generous choice of texts offered.

SAILLET, MAURICE. Appendix. In *Le Voleur de Talan,* by Pierre Reverdy. Paris: Flammarion, 1967. Valuable comments upon the source of this work and Reverdy's new typography.

SCHROEDER, JEAN P. "The Theme of Movement in the Poetry of Pierre Reverdy." Ph.D. dissertation, City University of New York, 1975.

SOMVILLE, LEON. "Les Romans autobiographiques de Pierre Reverdy." *Etudes Littéraires* 3, no. 1 (April, 1970), 21–45. Autobiographical references in *Le Voleur de Talan.*

STOJKOVIC, EMMA. *L'Oeuvre poétique de Pierre Reverdy.* Milan: Casa Editrice Dott. Antonio, 1951. General summary of thematic and stylistic comments on the early prose poems, on the thematic content of the later work; discussion of the poem as object ("poème-objet").

2. Related Studies

APOLLINAIRE, GUILLAUME. *Calligrammes, Poésie.* 1918; reprint Paris: Gallimard, 1975. A collection of poems, many of which are freely arranged on the page so as to produce a graphic representation.

BALAKIAN, ANNA. *The Literary Origins of Surrealism.* New York: New York University Press, 1947. An excellent study of the development of surrealism with particular emphasis on the background provided by German romanticism and the poetry of Baudelaire, Rimbaud, and Mallarmé, and the contributions of Apollinaire, the dadaists, Lautréamont, and Reverdy.

————. "The Surrealist Image." *The Romanic Review* 44, no. 4 (December, 1953), 273–81. An informative discussion of the characteristics of surrealist images and the different interpretations of the image in the aesthetics of Reverdy and Breton.

————. *Surrealism: The Road to the Absolute.* 1959; reprint. New York: E. P. Dutton, 1970. Another excellent study treating in further detail the affiliation of Lautréamont, Apollinaire, and Reverdy with surrealism, as well as the objectives Breton sought to reach with regard to poetic language, automatic writing, and imagery.

BAUDELAIRE, CHARLES. *Les Fleurs du mal.* 1957; reprint. Paris: Gallimard, 1964. A collection of poems in which Baudelaire like Reverdy is preoccupied with the theme of the voyage which is often associated with death.

BERGMAN, PAR. *Modernolatria et Simultaneità.* N.p.: Svenska Bokforlaget/ Bonniers, 1962. In depth study of the development of simultanism and futurism.

BRETON, ANDRE. *Manifestes du surréalisme.* Paris: Gallimard, 1924. Breton's manifestos which set forth his own interpretations concerning the philosophy of the surrealist movement and surrealist imagery, with particular attention to Reverdy's image theory.

CARROUGES, MICHEL. *André Breton et les données fondamentales du surréalisme.* Paris: Gallimard, 1950. Thorough study of the development of surrealism, with emphasis upon the influence of Rimbaud, Mallarmé, and Reverdy.

GOLDING, JOHN. *Le Cubisme*. Translated by Françoise Cachin. Paris: René Julliard, 1962. Excellent, detailed study of the evolution of cubism with well-selected illustrations.

KAMBER, GERALD. *Max Jacob and the Poetics of Cubism*. Baltimore: John Hopkins Press, 1971. An informative study of the different aspects of cubism as related to the work of Max Jacob.

LEMAITRE, GEORGES. *From Cubism to Surrealism in French Literature*. New York: Russell & Russell, 1941. A general study of the different phases of cubism and surrealism with a brief treatment of the contributions of the symbolists and futurists as well as a short analysis of related poetry such as that of Reverdy, Apollinaire, and Jacob among others.

MALLARME, STEPHANE. *Oeuvres complètes*. Edited by Henri Mondor and G. Jean-Aubry. Paris: Gallimard, 1945. The complete works of Mallarmé with poems treating several themes later found in the poetry of Reverdy: the voyage and flight from sterility, inauthenticity of language, and the shelter and protection of the fold.

MEAD, GERALD. *The Surrealist Image: A Stylistic Study*. New Haven: Yale University Press, 1971. An excellent study of the surrealist image as it has evolved under the influence of Marinetti and the futurists, Reverdy, and Breton.

NERVAL, GERARD DE. *Aurélia*. 1885; reprint. Paris: Librairie José Corti, 1964. A work of poetic prose in which the poet is haunted by specters of death and disintegration, later an obsession with Reverdy.

PONGE, FRANCIS. *Le Savon*. Paris: Gallimard, 1967. A play in which emphasis is placed upon the need to remove arbitrary, socially imposed connotations from words in order to arrive at true, poetic meaning.

RIMBAUD, ARTHUR. *Poésies complètes*. Paris: Gallimard, 1963. A collection of poetry, many texts of which treat the theme of descent, reappearing later in the poetry of Reverdy.

SARTRE, JEAN-PAUL. *L'Homme et les choses*. Paris: Seghers, 1947. An essay commenting on Ponge's theory of language, particularly his description of the "act of becoming" . . . that is, the realization of the existence of a term, independent of arbitrary, utilitarian meaning.

SERULLAZ, MAURICE. *Le Cubisme*. Paris: Presses Universitaires de France, 1963. Extremely informative study of the entire cubist movement in art, including a background of pre-cubist art, the various phases of the movement, and the most important cubist artists and their work, and finally, the art that followed cubism.

SOLLERS, PHILIPPE. *Entretiens de Francis Ponge avec Philippe Sollers*. Paris: Gallimard/Editions du Seuil, 1970. A series of interviews in which Ponge comments upon the need to purify language of its arbitrarily assigned connotations.

Index